Action research for educational change

Developing Teachers and Teaching

Series Editor: **Christopher Day,** Reader in Education Management and Director of Advanced Post-Graduate Courses in the School of Education, University of Nottingham.

Teachers and schools will wish not only to survive but also to flourish in a period which holds increased opportunities for self-management – albeit within centrally designed guidelines – combined with increased public and professional accountability. Each of the authors in this series provides perspectives which will both challenge and support practitioners at all levels who wish to extend their critical skills, qualities and knowledge of schools, pupils and teachers.

Current titles:

Angela Anning: *The First Years at School (second edition)*
Joan Dean: *Professional Development in School*
John Elliott: *Action Research for Educational Change*
Patrick Whitaker: *Managing Change in Schools*

Action research for educational change

John Elliott

Open University Press
Milton Keynes · Philadelphia

Open University Press
Celtic Court
22 Ballmoor
Buckingham
MK18 1XW

email: enquiries@openup.co.uk
world wide web: www.openup.co.uk

and
325 Chestnut Street
Philadelphia, PA 19106, USA

First Published 1991.
Reprinted 1992 (twice), 1993, 1996, 1997, 1998, 2001

A catalogue record of this book is available from the British Library

Library of Congress Cataloguing-in-Publication Data

Elliott, John, Dip. Phil. Ed.
    Action research for educational change / John Elliott.
       p. cm.—(Developing teachers and teaching series)
    Includes bibliographical references (p.   ) and index.
    ISBN 0–335–09689–1 (paperback)—ISBN 0–335–09690–5 (hardback)
    1. Action research in education—Great Britain.
    I. Title. II. Series.
    LB1028.24.E45   1991
    370′78041—dc20   90–14193
                                               CIP

Typeset by Rowland Phototypesetting Ltd
Bury St Edmunds, Suffolk
Printed and bound in Great Britain by
Biddles Ltd, www.biddles.co.uk

Contents

List of figures and tables

Acknowledgements

I am grateful to Pergamon Press for permission to reproduce a slightly amended version of my paper 'Teachers as researchers: implications for supervision and for teacher education', which was published in *Teaching and Teacher Education*, vol. 6, no. 1, 1990. This paper constitutes the substance of Chapters 1 and 2.

Thanks are also due to the Trustees of the Lawrence Stenhouse Memorial Trust for permission to reproduce the first Stenhouse Memorial Lecture, as Chapter 9.

Finally, I would like to acknowledge the contribution of the teachers and colleagues I have worked with over the years. For the ideas developed in this book I owe a special debt to Clem Adelman, Wilf Carr, Dave Ebutt, Stephen Kemmis, Barry MacDonald, Christine O'Hanlon, Helen Simons, Bridget Somekh and Brian Wakeman.

However, they will understand if I cite the late Lawrence Stenhouse as the person who exercised the greatest influence on the development of the ideas expressed in this book. Most of them can be traced back to him, although I like to believe that I have woven my own web with them.

Series editor's introduction

This book is about action research as a form of teacher professional development. It begins with the emergence of action research in the context of school initiated change in the 1960s (Chapter 1) and goes on to look at the methodological issues of facilitating it as a form of professional learning in schools (Chapter 2). The case studies in Chapter 2 are based on the author's own experience as a facilitator in three projects spanning over a decade and a half from 1967 to 1983. During that period he was located in higher-education institutions which have played a major role in sustaining the teachers-as-researchers movement within the UK. Yet he experienced the tensions between the clashing professional cultures of teachers and academics. Chapters 3, 4 and 5 focus on action-research as a 'cultural innovation' with transformative possibilities for both the professional culture of teachers and teacher educators in academe. They attempt to identify some of the problems of effecting this transformation, and thereby resolving the theory–practice issue (see Chapter 3) which has bedevilled discussions about the role of higher-education institutions in the professional development of teachers. Elliott claims that we are now at a point where policy initiatives are denying the value of that role.

The 'resolution' of the theory–practice issue is being shaped by government initiatives which are essentially part of a new technology of surveillance and control over teachers' practices in classrooms and schools. Within this technology the role of the teacher is in danger of being deprofessionalized and reduced to that of a supervised technical operative. The tasks of educators become specialized and hierarchized.

Chapter 4 describes such a development which is destabilizing and eroding the traditional craft culture of teachers. But in doing so it is creating the conditions for the spread of a more reflective culture, which emerges as a form of creative resistance to the technical rationality that underpins government policy-making. It seems that one of the unintended effects of government interventions in education is to create the conditions for a resolution of the theory–practice issue and the emergence of a form of professional development grounded in action research. But the promise is as yet largely unfulfilled. It remains a popular aspiration.

Chapter 5 examines some of the dilemmas teachers confront while doing research in schools as part of a higher-education course. Elliott looks at some examples of the ways which these dilemmas are resolved to reinforce the assumptions that underpin both the traditional craft culture in schools and the traditional research culture in higher-education institutions. The theory–practice divide gets perpetuated rather than resolved by the compromises and trade-offs. The development of an authentic methodology of reflective practice, which is not simply derivative of outsider research methodologies, is in its infancy. A thousand flowers may be blooming, but without vigilance they can die.

Chapter 6 is a practical guide to action research. It has been used with teachers, and Elliott still has some doubts. Viewed in retrospect, the chapter seems to represent the reflective process too mechanically, as a set of sequenced steps. Teachers drew this to his attention. It was his unconscious trade-off with the new technology of education. He is also aware that the techniques suggested are somewhat, although not exclusively, derived from outsider research methodologies. So, the chapter should be viewed critically, as a guide to test against experience rather than as an authoritative prescription. Chapter 6 suggests a resolution of the 'development v. accountability' issue. Action research is a means of demonstrating, to parents and schools governors, the steps one has taken to improve practice in classrooms and schools.

The final three chapters look at three specific policy contexts in which action research as a form of professional learning has to be forged in the future: the national curriculum, teacher appraisal, and competence-based teacher training. With respect to each, Elliott suggests, higher education appears to have a diminishing role. He outlines alternative models of curriculum, appraisal, and competence-based training and indicates the central role action research would play in fostering teaching quality within these frameworks.

Whilst Elliott claims that he is not over-optimistic about the future of action research as a mode of professional learning, Chapter 7 lays the grounds for some optimism, elaborating upon his theory of creative resistance.

Since the 1960s, the action-research movement has grown and spread in England and around the world. It has become a clarion call for all those who believe in learning through reflecting 'where the action is', wherever their workplace. John Elliott has played initiating and leading roles at all levels in promoting this; and this book provides invaluable insights for all who are engaged in professional development.

Christopher Day

Part I

Action research and professional learning

Part II

Teachers as researchers: an historical and biographical context

Drawing on his experience as a teacher in the 1960s, the author argues that action research emerged as an aspect of the school-based curriculum reforms in the secondary modern schools. In doing so he attempts to counter the popular view that the teachers-as-researchers movement was initiated by academics in the higher-education sector.

The chapter concludes with an account of the educational theories that underpinned the curriculum practices of innovatory teachers in the 1960s. The author shows how the idea of action research is implied by the educational theories embedded in teacher-initiated curriculum reform.

The teachers-as-researchers movement emerged in England during the 1960s. Its context was essentially that of curriculum reform within a differentiated educational system. At the age of 11 children were allocated to either grammar or secondary modern schools on the basis of tests known as the eleven-plus. The grammar-school curriculum was essentially subject-based and the syllabuses were orientated towards public examinations at 16, in the form of the General Certificate of Education (GCE). Grammar-school students then faced a choice of whether they left school for a job or proceeded to take certain GCE subjects for a further two years to secure advanced-level passes, which together with their ordinary-level passes would secure entrance into a university. Those who failed the eleven-plus, the vast majority of students, followed a watered-down subject-based curriculum. A small proportion of these proceeded to take GCE ordinary-level examinations at 16. The rest took either no public examinations at all or examinations which were considered to have inferior status to GCE. The national school-leaving age was 15, and many students left without taking any public examinations at all.

I began my teaching career in a secondary modern school in the early 60s as a religious-education and biology specialist. The Education Act of 1944 made religion a compulsory curriculum subject. In fact it was the only subject secondary schools were legally obliged to provide. However, the system of public examinations ensured a broad conformity of curriculum provision. The control over the curriculum exerted through public examinations was greatest in the grammar schools. But the content of GCE syllabuses was reflected in the curriculum framework of the secondary moderns. The GCE syllabuses were devised and the examinations set and marked, by a number of university-controlled examination boards.

Large numbers of students in the secondary modern schools were alienated from the 'watered-down' academic curriculum they followed. They were destined to emerge from their schooling as failures, with the exception of the few who could cope sufficiently to compensate for their failure to pass the eleven-plus test by taking the GCE examinations at ordinary level. (The secondary moderns generally did not make provision for advanced levels.) The grouping practices of the secondary moderns tended to reflect those of the grammar schools. On entry students were grouped into 'streams' according to 'academic ability' and, although in theory movement across was possible, it happened rarely in practice. Students' opportunities for success were largely determined by the streaming system, although the alternative grouping practice of 'subject setting' was adopted in many schools to rectify the perceived deficiencies of the system. 'Setting' was essentially a system of streaming on a subject rather than a cross-curricular basis and normally applied to only a certain range of academically high-status subjects in the upper part of the 11–16 age range. It tended to operate more in the grammar than the secondary modern schools, because its major purpose was to give above-average students opportunities to maximize their number of GCE subject passes.

Knowing that they were destined within the system to fail, large numbers of students in the secondary moderns lacked any interest in the subject-matter of the curriculum. Their slim chances of securing examination success meant that examinations were a poor extrinsic motivator. The alienation was particularly acute in those humanities subjects which students and their parents perceived to have little relevance to the world of work: namely, history, geography and religion.

Faced with both passive resistance and active rebellion, teachers in the secondary moderns had two choices. The first was to develop and maintain a system of coercive control: to turn secondary moderns into 'concentration camps'. The second was to make the curriculum more intrinsically interesting for the students and transform the examination system to reflect such a change.

During the 60s the secondary moderns began to vary somewhat in their ethos. At one end of a continuum were the 'concentration camps' and at the other the quite recognizable 'innovatory secondary moderns', with the majority of schools in between, struggling with an internal tension between these two climates. I was fortunate in beginning my teaching career during 1962 in a school which was beginning to emerge at the innovatory end of this continuum.

The emergence of the curriculum-reform movement

During my period in the school we destreamed and created mixed-ability groups. Curriculum reform focused on the teaching of the humanities subjects of English, history, geography and religion in the fourth and fifth years. At first they operated within subject boundaries. But teachers across these subjects shared the common aspirations of enabling students to make connections between the subject-matter and their everyday experience. In each subject area content was selected and organized around life-themes such as 'the family', 'relations between the sexes', 'war and society', 'education', 'the world of work', 'law and order', 'the media', etc. Experience taught us that we could not help students explore these themes in depth by maintaining a subject-based form of curriculum organization. Students experienced a great deal of repetition as they moved from one subject to another. What went on in English didn't appear so very different from what went on in history, geography or religious studies. We began to realize that content from the different subject areas needed to be employed eclectically by students in terms of its perceived relevance to questions and issues as they emerged in the classroom. Separate time slots were beginning to look disfunctional, and teachers needed to draw on each others' subject expertise. So we created 'integrated studies' and worked together in cross-subject teams. Similar developments were taking place in a number of secondary moderns across England and Wales.

Implicit in this school-based curriculum-reform movement were newly emergent conceptions of learning, teaching and evaluation which were ex-plicated in justificatory discourse as the innovatory teachers attempted to negotiate collaborative activities with each other, and to justify them to their more traditionalist colleagues in staffrooms. I well remember the lay-out in the staffroom of my school: a large oval arrangement of easy chairs around the gas-fire. There over coffee we sat during breaks discussing and debating our attempts to bring about change with colleagues who regarded our ideas with some scepticism. The quality of this curriculum discourse was an experience which has influenced all my subsequent thinking and action as an educationalist.

From the standpoint of my own professional life-history the activity of curriculum theorizing was something I initially encountered amongst teachers in a school. The 'theories' of learning, teaching and evaluation we articulated in staffroom gatherings and meetings derived from our attempts to bring about change in a particular set of circumstances, rather than from our professional training in universities and colleges of education. They were not so much applications of educational theory learned in the world of academe, but generations of theory from attempts to change curriculum practice in the school. Theory was derived from practice and constituted a set of abstractions from it. This view of the theory–practice relationship was quite contrary to the rationalist assumptions built into teacher training at the time: namely, that good practice consists of the application of theoretical knowledge and principles which are consciously understood prior to it.

I learned as a teacher that theories were implicit in all practices, and that theorizing consisted of articulating those 'tacit theories' and subjecting them to critique in free and open professional discourse. I also learned that high-quality professional discourse depends upon the willingness of everyone involved to tolerate a diversity of views and practices. In my school there was certainly an identifiable group of teachers who could be described as 'the innovators'. But we never became a self-contained and exclusive club or an isolated rebel clique, so we never established an impermeable dogmatism.

There were a number of reasons for this. First, the staff group was a relatively small one of around 25 teachers. This maximized opportunities for each individual to have frequent face-to-face interactions with everyone else. So we got to know each other as persons pretty well. We played cricket, golf and football with each other, socialized together after school and at week-ends, and collaborated in out-of-school activities with students. This knowledge of each other as persons did much to foster free, open and tolerant professional discourse.

Second, the headteacher refrained from using his own power position to impose change on the staff. He had a broad vision of the direction in which he wanted things to go, and everyone was aware of it. They were aware that his sympathies were with the views of the innovators. But he did not put himself forward as the authoritative curriculum theorist, or as the major initiator of reforms. He identified issues and problems and then encouraged staff to develop their own change proposals. He then supported the implementation of proposals, if certain conditions were complied with. One condition was that participation by staff in change should be voluntary. Another was that the innovation should be monitored and evaluated, and accounts of its effects rendered to the staff as a whole.

The headteacher's management practices did much to make the staff at the traditionalist end of the spectrum feel that they were not entirely powerless to exert leverage over the nature, direction and pace of change. And they did much to ensure that the innovators felt under an obligation to communicate and justify their practices to the whole staff group. What the headteacher did was to foster a collegial system of intra-professional accountability grounded in reflective practice.

One example of the headteacher's management style was the introduction of mixed-ability grouping. Streaming had become a controversial issue in the school. He responded by organizing a series of staff meetings on the subject. Rather than present his own arguments against streaming or inviting a member of staff to do so, he invited a major researcher at the reputable National Foundation for Educational Research to address the staff. By the end of the series of meetings the general feeling amongst the staff was that streaming in the school was having undesirable effects. But many were anxious about a change to mixed-ability grouping. Some argued that 'bright' children would be disadvantaged, while others doubted their ability to cope with the 'less able' in this setting. The headteacher suggested that a one-year pilot experiment should be established with the first years and thoroughly monitored by all the staff prior to any decision about establishing mixed groups throughout the school. At the end of the pilot experiment the vast majority of teachers were prepared for whole-school innovation, but the head of the maths department still held out for grouping according to ability. So it was decided that the maths groups would be organized in ability sets.

I have attempted to describe those contextual factors which contributed to the quality of curriculum discourse in my school. They pick out a personal and a structural dimension. We had opportunities to get to know one another as persons beyond the boundaries of our professional roles. But we also had a management structure which supported a 'bottom up' rather than a 'top down' change process, and a collegial rather than an individualistic or bureaucratic form of accountability, i.e. accountability to peers as opposed to accountability to oneself alone or to a superordinate.

Handy (1984) claims that management systems threaten the professional autonomy of practitioners when policy is both generated and executed hierarchically. He argues that management systems which establish collegial structures for policy generation but retain hierarchical structures for executing policy are likely to find acceptance amongst professionals. Certainly the management of change in my school reflected this separation of policy generation from executive roles. In fact the deputy headteachers were at the traditionalist end of the spectrum. But this was not a tremendous problem for the change agents in the school, because the deputy headteachers had very little control over the generation and development of curriculum policies.

From the standpoint of my professional life-history I first participated in educational research, as well as curriculum theorizing, as a teacher in my school. Theorizing about practice was not an activity conducted in isolation from researching our practice. For example, we frequently debated whether students were able at 14 years of age to reflect meaningfully about adult experience. Some argued that these students were not in a position to grasp the meaning of certain adult experiences because they had not reached an appropriate stage of emotional development. We didn't resolve such issues by citing theories of adolescent development contained in the psychological research literature, although some of us might have employed them from time to time when defending our own 'theories of readiness' or trying to undermine those of others. Instead, we searched for evidence in our practices within the school.

Curriculum practices were not derived from curriculum theories generated and tested independently of that practice. They constituted the means by which we generated and tested our own and each others' theories. Practices took on the status of hypotheses to be tested. So we collected empirical data about their effects, and used it as evidence in which to ground our theorizing with each other in a context of collegial accountability. We didn't call it research, let alone action-research. This articulation came much later as the world of academia responded to change in schools. But the concept of teaching as reflexive practice and a form of educational inquiry was tacitly and intuitively grasped in our experience of the innovation process. Our research was by no means systematic. It occurred as a response to particular questions and issues as they arose. Let me illustrate the process.

The deputy head in charge of the pastoral care of girls organized an event in which the fourth-year girls were shown a film depicting the birth of a baby in great detail. Letters requesting parental permission for showing the film had been sent out well in advance. By lunch-time on the day of the showing, word got around the staff-room that four girls had simultaneously fainted during the showing. I remember arguing that it would never have happened if the boys had been there to provide an emotional check on this chain reaction.

During the afternoon the boys in my fourth-year class complained about not being able to see the film. They claimed the girls were using the occasion to impute 'emotional immaturity' to them, an explanation for exclusion the girls had evidently obtained from the female deputy head. I decided to test this gender-based theory of 'emotional maturity' (perhaps against my own equally gender-based one) by inviting all fourth-year boys to see the film in the geography room after school and any girls who wished to view it again. A large number of boys and girls turned up. No immature behaviour was evidenced from the boys, no girls fainted, and the showing was followed by a thoughtful, lively, and sensitive discussion.

However, at one point the film was interrupted by the entrance of the male deputy head who told me to stop it. He argued that it was not suitable for the boys to watch and feared problems would arise since they had not been given as thorough a preparation as the girls had. The school, he argued, could not defend my action since parental permission had not been granted for the boys to view it. I had offended against school procedures. I argued that everything was going well and that it would be counterproductive to stop the film now.

The next morning the headteacher called me into his study and told me I had upset both his deputies. He reprimanded me for going against the established procedures, and then in the same breath praised me for having such a 'good idea'. He then asked me to lead a discussion with a mixed-sex group of fourth years in the school hall that morning. The aim was to elicit their views on the kind of sex education they wanted in the school. The headteacher told me that he intended to slip into the hall to listen after the discussion had begun to flow naturally and smoothly.

The data we gathered during these events, from observation of practice and student feed-back, provided the basis for changes in the sex-education pro-gramme within the school. Moreover, the data processing did not take place against a background of routinized and predictable practices. The practice shifted as the data was processed. Information about the fainting episode led me to hypothesize that it wouldn't have happened in the presence of boys. The feed-back from the boys about their feelings on being excluded prompted me to organize the second showing in order to test the hypotheses that the girls wouldn't faint in the presence of the boys, and that the boys wouldn't display immature behaviour in the presence of girls. The success of the second showing then stimulated the gathering of further data from students about their needs in the area of sex education.

I wouldn't claim that this is a good example of rigorous educational inquiry. But it does illustrate a process in which ideas are tested and developed in action. I would argue that this form of teachers-based action research is a characteristic feature of a certain kind of curriculum-reform process. Let me therefore try to summarize, on the basis of my experience, what these characteristics are:

1 It is a process which is initiated by practising teachers in response to a particular practical situation they confront.
2 The practical situation is one in which their traditional curriculum practices have been destabilized and rendered problematic by the development of student resistance or 'refusal to learn'.
3 The innovations proposed arouse controversy within the staff group, be-cause they challenge the fundamental beliefs embodied in existing practices about the nature of learning, teaching and evaluation.
4 Issues are clarified and resolved in free and open collegial discourse, characterized by mutual respect and tolerance for others' views, in the absence of power constraints on the discussion's outcomes.
5 Change proposals are treated as provisional hypotheses to be tested in practice within a context of collegial accountability to the whole staff group.
6 The management facilitates a 'bottom-up' rather than a 'top-down' approach to the development of curriculum policies and strategies.

The curriculum theory of the curriculum-reform movement

This kind of curriculum-reform process is not theoretically neutral. It is guided by a cluster of interrelated ideas about the nature of education, knowledge, learning, curriculum and teaching. These ideas become articulated and clari-fied in the process. Education is no longer viewed as a process of adapting or accommodating the mind to structures of knowledge. Instead it is viewd as a dialectical process in which the meaning and significance of structures are reconstructed in the historically conditioned consciousness of individuals as they try to make sense of their 'life situations'. The mind 'adapts with' rather than 'adapts to' structures of knowledge.

This view of education implies a shift in the concept of learning which in turn shifts the criteria by which it is assessed. Learning is viewed as the active production rather than the passive reproduction of meaning. Its outcomes are no longer to be assessed in terms of the match between inputs and predetermined output criteria, but rather in terms of the intrinsic qualities of being they manifest. When learning is viewed as 'active production', then it becomes a manifestation of human powers, e.g. to synthesize disparate and complex information into coherent patterns, to look at situations from different points of view, to self-monitor personal bias and prejudice, etc. The development of understanding is construed as the extension of the students' natural powers in relation to the things which matter in life. The manifestation of such qualities can be described and judged but not standardized and measured.

The idea of teaching embedded in the change process is also different. It is no longer construed as an activity aimed at controlling or casually determining the outcomes of learning. Rather it is viewed as an enabling activity which aims to facilitate an indeterminate dialectical process between public structures of knowledge and individual subjectivities. Its focus is on the process rather than the product of learning. It is directed towards activating, engaging, challenging and stretching the natural powers of the human mind.

The criteria for evaluating teaching refer to the extent to which teachers provide students with opportunities for manifesting and enhancing these powers. The criteria for evaluating learning and teaching are distinct. The former refer to the qualities of mind manifested in learning outcomes. The latter refer to the extent to which the pedagogy is an enabling rather than a constraining influence on students' opportunities to manifest and develop these qualities. Such a pedagogy requires teachers to reflect in as well as on the classroom process quite independently from any assessment they make of the quality of learning outcomes. Pedagogy is a reflective process. It is process rather than product data which forms the basis of evaluations of teaching. And a major source of that data will be the students themselves: their accounts of the respects in which teaching enables or constrains the development of their powers in relation to the things which matter.

All this contrasts with the criteria of teacher evaluation implicit in the idea that teaching is about controlling or determining learning outcomes. Such criteria are the same as those governing the evaluation of learning: namely, specifications of desired outputs. If a student's performance fails to match the output specification, then responsibility for such a 'defect' is ascribed to the teaching. Evaluating teaching from the perspective of the product model does not involve grounding judgements in subjective data about students' perceptions of teaching within the pedagogical process. Although teachers will reflect *on* their practice in the light of its outcomes, they will not reflect on it in process. In this sense teaching will not constitute in itself a reflective practice.

The final conceptual shift involved in the curriculum-reform process described is in the view of the relationship between curriculum and teaching. The curriculum is not seen as an organized selection of knowledge, concepts and skills determined independently of the pedagogical process, solely on the basis of public structures of knowledge. Rather, the curriculum map is shaped within pedagogical practice as the teacher selects and organizes 'knowledge content' in response to students' own search for meaning, and then monitors their responses in the light of such criteria as 'relevant to their concerns', 'interesting', 'challenging', and 'stretching'. Students' subjective experiences constitute the data, in the light of which the teacher adjusts and modifies the emerging map. As the map unfolds and is pedagogically validated in retrospect through self-monitoring, it enables the teacher to anticipate but not predict future possibilities. It provides the teacher with a sense of direction without prescribing a fixed agenda.

As an aspect of a reflective pedagogy the curriculum is always in the process of becoming. It is developed in and through the pedagogical process. The activity of validating the developing map within the classroom process entails a reflective pedagogy. Validating the curriculum-in-process requires the teacher to appraise all the dimensions of both pedagogy and its context. The teacher has to sort out whether indications that the students are not engaged with, or stretched by, the content can be explained by the inappropriateness of the material and its organization or by other factors, e.g. the way the teacher structures and handles student responses, or institutional and psychological constraints on self-directed and active learning. This requires a great deal of self-reflection and experimentation. Understanding and diagnosing the problem situation is not an instant event. The action implications of explanatory hypotheses about constraining factors within the pedagogy and its context have to be explored and evaluated before one can conclude that the selection and organization of content is operating as a significant constraint on learning.

I have tried to describe the cluster of theoretical ideas embedded, with varying degrees of explicitness, in the curriculum-change process I participated in within my secondary modern school. This curriculum-change process emerged in the 60s in a number of innovatory secondary modern schools. The prospect of the raising of the school-leaving age from 15 to 16 years was a great impetus from the mid-60s for a radical rethink of the curriculum for the so-called average- and below-average-ability student. The development of a new teacher-controlled public examination at sixteen-plus, the Certificate of Secondary Education, also enabled teachers to construct examinations which reflected the aspirations of the curriculum reformers.

As selection at eleven-plus was replaced by the reorganization of secondary schools into comprehensive institutions, the change process was considerably diluted. The secondary moderns either merged with grammar schools or were developed into comprehensives. The old grammar-school view of education, knowledge, learning, and teaching, dominated the new institutions. They felt under political pressure to justify their existence against grammar-school 'standards'. From the turn of the decade we witnessed what Hargreaves (1982) has described as the 'grammarization' of the comprehensive school. However, the 'curriculum theory' became a continuing, if subordinate, aspect of the professional culture of secondary teachers.

2

Supporting professional learning through action research: three case studies

The chapter contains three case studies of action-research projects which the author has been involved with as an external facilitator. It uses the case studies to explore the problem of how outsider researchers from higher education can facilitate 'insider research' in schools, without fostering dependence on the 'academic authority' of the former. The case studies explore some major methodological issues about how to facilitate the professional learning of teachers through action research. They illustrate a second-order process of action research by the author, i.e. a process of reflectively analysing his experience as an action-research facilitator.

'Hijacking' teachers' theories: the academic word game

I have spent a considerable amount of space mapping out a curriculum-change process in which I participated over 20 years ago because I have spent my subsequent professional life as a teacher educator and educational researcher, articulating and elaborating on the theoretical ideas which underpinned it. I wanted to make it clear that the theoretical origins of my work with teachers on various action-research projects lay in my experience of a certain kind of innovatory curriculum practice in schools. My theoretical understanding of education, knowledge, learning and teaching are not so much derived from an academic culture which adopts a contemplative stance towards the process of schooling, as from curriculum practices in which I participated as a teacher with my peers. If these understandings are now widely shared aspects of the academic culture in schools of teacher education, it is because teacher educators have appropriated them from practice.

Ideas which subsequently emerged in academia like 'there can be no curriculum development without teacher development', 'teaching as a form of educational research', 'teachers as researchers', and 'educational action research', all encapsulate certain dimensions of the curriculum practice I have described. But they describe that practice in the language of academe. Naturalistic reflection in and on the pedagogical process becomes described as 'research'. Assumptions underpinning such academic language have tended to distort the process. All too often research is viewed as something teachers now do *on* their practice. They step out of their pedagogical role. Teaching and research become posited as separate activities, whereas from the standpoint of the practitioner reflection and action are simply two aspects of a single process. Having translated 'reflection' or 'self-evaluation' into 'research', the academic is in danger of interpreting methodology as a set of mechanical procedures and standardized techniques rather than as a cluster of dynamic ideas and principles which structure, but do not determine, the search for understanding within the pedagogical process. The separation of 'research' from 'teaching' implies a separation between teaching and curriculum development. The idea of developing the curriculum through teaching presupposes a unified concept of teaching as a reflective practice.

Rather than playing the role of the theoretical handmaiden of practitioners by helping them to clarify, test, develop and disseminate the ideas which underpin their practices, academics tend to behave like terrorists. We take an idea which underpins teachers' practices, distort it through translation into 'academic jargon', and thereby 'hijack' it from its practical context and the web of interlocking ideas which operate within that context. And so we find teacher educators and educational researchers propagating ideas like 'educational action research', and 'teachers as researchers' as if they could be *applied* to any sort of practice in schools, regardless of teachers' conceptions of education, knowledge, learning and teaching, and regardless of the institutional and social context of their practices.

All too often the idea that educational inquiry constitutes a form of teaching and vice versa gets lost. In Britain we now have numerous award-bearing and research-based in-service courses for teachers. Action research and the 'teachers as researchers' movement are now enthusiastically promoted in academia. But the question is this: are the academics transforming the methodology of teacher-based educational inquiry into a form which enables them to manipulate and control teachers' thinking in order to reproduce the central assumptions which have underpinned a contemplative academic culture detached from the practices of everyday life?

I know that I have often colluded in acts of academic imperialism. These first two chapters are an attempt to return to the experiential origins of my ideas, in the hope that this reflexive process will help me to avoid the distorting effects of an over-immersion in academia. It is not that I feel my professional life as an academic has not helped me to deepen my understanding of educational practice. It gives me access to ideas which indeed challenge the very assumptions which have underpinned teacher education and educational research. The academic culture is not homogeneous and embodies its own counterculture. Nevertheless the institutional structures which impinge on my daily practice continue to sustain and support conceptions of 'excellence' and 'standards' which make it difficult for me to initiate and sustain forms of practice as a supervisor and educational researcher which embody different conceptions of these terms.

The institutionalization of 'action research' and 'teachers as researchers' as approaches to teacher education within academic institutions raises a number of critical issues for tutors and supervisors to reflect about. If we are to facilitate reflective practice as a form of educational inquiry in schools, then we must treat teacher education as a reflective practice also.

In the rest of this chapter I shall try to identify some of the ways in which teacher educators have tended to distort and constrain the development of the reflective practice they aspired to promote. I will do so by reflecting on my own experience as a teacher educator.

The Humanities Curriculum Project: support for reflective curriculum practice

In the summer of 1967 I joined a large curriculum-reform project initiated by the Schools Council, a national agency established in the mid-60s to support reform in the areas of curriculum and examinations. The Council had given an early priority to reforming the curriculum for students of 'average' and 'below average' academic ability in the humanities subjects. It had published two major working papers (numbers 2 and 11) on the problem prior to establishing the Humanities Project under the direction of Lawrence Stenhouse. The whole ethos of the Council was to support and disseminate the best innovatory practices in schools.

Stenhouse's contribution to the curriculum-reform movement was to articulate the paradigm of curriculum design which had emerged from the school-based curriculum-reform movement in embryo form. Central to this paradigm was the specification of a *praxiology*: a set of principles to guide teachers in translating educational aims into concrete pedagogical practices (see Stenhouse 1975 and Elliott 1983a). This praxiology (my term for such principles rather than Stenhouse's) embraced the process of education and not simply its content.

Reflecting the trend to focus on life themes as a basis for reorganizing curriculum content, Stenhouse's starting-point was to articulate a general aim for the study of such themes. The human situations and acts they referred to raised controversial value-issues within our society. So Stenhouse defined the aim of the humanities in education as 'developing an understanding of social situations and human acts and the controversial value issues which they raise'. He refused to analyse this aim into specific content objectives, a position which was entirely consistent with the theory of learning underpinning the curriculum-change process I outlined earlier. Instead he analysed the aim into a set of procedural principles governing the handling of information in classrooms. After R. S. Peters (1968), Stenhouse argued that from an educational aim one could logically derive a form of pedagogical process which was consistent with that aim. The principles which defined the pedagogical process in the context of the Humanities Project were as follows:

1 that controversial issues should be handled in the classroom with adolescents
2 that teachers should not use their authority as teachers as a platform for promoting their own views
3 that the mode of inquiry in controversial areas should have discussion rather than instruction at its core
4 that the discussion should protect divergence of view among participants
5 that the teacher as chairperson of the discussion should have responsibility for quality and standards in learning.

The teacher's role was to develop pedagogical strategies for realizing these principles within the classroom. Such strategies could not be determined in advance of the circumstances of their operation. The procedural principles were intended to orientate and guide teaching but not to prescribe concrete action strategies in the form of rules. Stenhouse believed such strategies were highly context dependent. It is possible to generalize strategies from past experience in a range of situations but their applicability to any future set of classroom circumstances had to be examined *in situ*. Such generalizations constitute practical hypotheses to be tested in particular pedagogical settings rather than sets of prescriptive rules.

Pedagogy conceived, after Stenhouse, as attempts to realize procedural principles in concrete practical form is necessarily a reflective process. *Praxiology* cannot be translated into *praxis* independently of the teacher's reflection and deliberation in particular situations. Moreover, praxis, as a set of strategic acts for realizing the procedural principles of humanites teaching, cannot be divorced from the curriculum. The curriculum is not a body of predetermined static content to be reproduced via the pedagogical process. Rather it is the selection and organization of content within a dynamic and reflective pedagogical process and is therefore constantly evolved and developed through it. Pedagogy takes the form of an experimental process of curriculum inquiry. Hence the centrality of the idea of teachers as researchers in Stenhouse's view of curriculum development. He claimed that there could be no curriculum development without teacher development and by this he meant the development of teachers' reflective capacities.

In a review of Stenhouse's book *An Introduction to Curriculum Research and Development* (1975) in *The Times Educational Supplement*, David Jenkins described the author as a 'chess player in a world of draughts'. Certainly his thinking went beyond the prevailing conventions. In the world of academe he upset those academics smitten with the objectives or product model of curriculum development where aims are analysed into content objectives to provide a basis for selecting and organizing predetermined content. Stenhouse argued that curriculum development was not a process which preceded the pedagogy, and pedagogy was not the technical process of transmitting curriculum content to achieve pre-specified learning outcomes.

In the world of teachers Stenhouse upset those traditionalists who were committed to the view that education is about the reproduction of knowledge content; a view which was unquestioned by academic enthusiasts for the product model. The traditionalists believed that teachers should use their authority to take sides on controversial issues in order to promote the right and correct point of view. More generally, they objected to Stenhouse's meddling with pedagogy, viewing his procedural principles as prescriptive and an infringement of the teacher's right to professional autonomy. In their view national curriculum projects should confine their efforts to mapping objectives and content. The role of such projects was to support curriculum change by providing resource materials for teachers to use. Develop the curriculum and let teachers decide how to implement it. Curriculum change was viewed as a process of changing the content rather than the process of education.

What these traditionalists, many of them serving on national committees of the Schools Council as representatives of teacher associations, failed to grasp was that Stenhouse's intrusion into the domain of pedagogy was based on a radical reinterpretation of the nature of the educational process and the relationships between its various elements. They also failed to grasp that he was doing no more than articulating, in a very comprehensive form, the logic of teachers' initiated curriculum reform. I doubt if Stenhouse himself fully appreciated this and so only exacerbated the problem of communication. His ideas appeared to originate beyond the teachers' practical 'horizon', somewhere in academia. In my view they originated within the 'horizons' of teachers, from an emergent curriculum-change process. The ideas emerged under the nose of the teaching profession, but many of its members failed to grasp them. They were perhaps so locked into their 'game of draughts' that they failed to appreciate that some of their peers at least were 'playing chess'.

Stenhouse was not the 'chess player'. His genius lay in his ability to penetrate at a stroke the logic which underpinned the new game some teachers were playing. But he tended to assume and convey the impression that the Humanities Project was a game he had invented rather than discovered. As I shall now explain, this assumption presented not only problems for communicating the project to teachers, but for conceptualizing the relationship between practitioners and teacher educators in the curriculum development process.

The central team of the Humanities Project appeared in some respects to fulfil the role teachers generally expected of curriculum developers. Initially we confined our attention to the production of materials. We edited multi-media packs of resource material on such themes as 'The Family', 'War and Society', 'Poverty'. These packs were then placed in volunteer trial schools, after a training seminar for the teachers involved. They were asked to assess the potential of the materials for supporting a process of discussion-based inquiry into controversial issues. Stenhouse viewed the role of the central team as less than ideal. It was, given the shortage of time leading up to the trials in schools, necessary to generate a foundation collection quickly. Teachers didn't have the time to produce it in a form which met the criteria set out below. However, it was hoped that as the classroom process became established they would continuously supplement and amend the foundation materials. The materials were edited in the light of the following criteria:

• The multi-media compilation should constitute selections from a variety of disciplines or arts.
• It should cover a wide range of controversial human acts.
• It should provide documentation of controversial issues from a variety of angles.
• It should support the exploration of controversial issues in depth.

No detailed guidance for using the material was issued. The items were simply listed and cross-referred to certain categories of human action, e.g. demonstrations, conscientious objection, killing, bombing cities. Teachers were not required to use particular items, and there was no prescribed sequence or path through the compilations. The selection and organization of the material were for teachers to judge in process.

As developers of resource materials from which teachers could select, our role as outsiders did not constitute any threat to teachers' professional autonomy within the pedagogical process. The problems between 'outsiders' and 'insiders' only began to emerge as teachers began to provide us with feedback on their use of materials. Although we had asked them to evaluate the extent to which the material supported the pedagogy, they tended to assume that their strategies for handling such material were non-problematic. They focused the critique on the materials rather than their context of use. When we raised questions about this context, they began to feel that we were stepping out of role and encroaching on their professional territory.

One very good example of the tension was the large amount of feedback teachers gave testifying to the difficulties students had in reading the material. An analysis of the feedback forms revealed little consensus amongst teachers on any single item in the compilations. This suggested that 'the context of use' might explain negative student reactions to the material better than 'reading difficulty'.

We were faced with a situation in which we had not presumed 'pedagogical competence' on the part of the teachers, but where they had expected us to make such a presumption. The materials-development team began to shift its focus from the production of material to the study of the pedagogical context in which it was being used. In relation to the 'reading difficulty' issue, for example, we observed classrooms, and interviewed students. The students frequently denied finding the material difficult and inaccessible for purposes of discussion. 'You can always get the gist of it, and then understand more as you discuss it,' was a typical response. The problem from the students' point of view was that teachers believed they couldn't comprehend the material and therefore spent a lot of time taking them through comprehension exercises before the material was discussed. 'You don't feel like discussing it after he has given you a hundred questions to answer about it first,' I remember one student explaining.

In the light of this kind of student feedback we began to observe two quite distinct patterns of information handling in classrooms:

1 READ — UNDERSTAND — DISCUSS
2 READ — DISCUSS — UNDERSTAND

Less students testified to reading difficulty when they experienced the second pattern.

In the light of growing evidence that teachers were not evaluating curriculum material in the context of the strategies they employed in handling it, the problem of externally supporting curriculum development in schools began to look very different. It was no longer simply a matter of producing materials for teachers to test in classrooms. It was also a matter of fostering the development of teachers' capacities for self-reflection. Providing feedback from our own observations and interviews was insufficient. From the teachers' point of view we were using the data we collected to mount a critique of their pedagogy. They suspected we were manipulating the data to these ends through the ways we collected, selected and interpreted it. But they felt powerless to defend themselves since, as busy practitioners, they were unable to create an independent data base.

The evaluation process in the classroom appeared to foster an unequal power relation between outsiders and insiders. No amount of feedback in this context will foster self-understandings generated from teachers' self-initiated reflection about their practices. Its effect, when not successfully resisted, is to create a situation in which practitioners come to depend on outsiders for their self-understandings.

The perception of outsiders' attempts to promote dependency was reinforced by their apparent superior knowledge of the criteria governing the analysis of data. Teachers experienced their practices as being judged against criteria defined by the development team, i.e. the principles of procedure. It could be argued that, if such criteria were genuinely implicit in teachers' conceptions of their aims, then they should be helped to articulate these for themselves as they reflected about strategies for realizing these aims. In other words, teachers should not only take responsibility for realizing a pedagogical theory in practice, but also for generating such a theory from practice. Within the central team of the Humanities Project we cast ourselves in the role of theory generators, and thereby tacitly reinforced an unequal power relation between ourselves and teachers. I shall return to this point again.

We were not insensitive to the power issue, being committed to the idea that successful curriculum change depended on the development of teachers' capacities for self-analysis and reflection. Attempts were made to resolve the problem I have outlined by establishing a form of collaborative classroom inquiry which promoted rather than constrained self-reflection.

Teachers were invited to tape-record their lessons and send selected recordings to the central team for analysis. This strategy ensured that the outsiders worked on data collected and selected by the teacher. It also reduced the amount of data we had access to, in comparison with the teachers, including access to very sensitive and threatening data about students' perceptions of the classroom and pedagogy. Each tape submitted was transcribed, and the transcript analysed by a member of the central team. The analyses, with the transcripts, were returned to the teachers for comment. They took the form of hypotheses about the problems and potential of the pedagogy for realizing the procedural principles. Teachers were asked to explore these hypotheses in relation to their own classroom practices.

This collaborative strategy tended to reduce the anxiety level and consequent defensiveness of teachers. Not only did they exercise more control over our access to data, but they were able to treat our analyses of it as genuinely hypothetical. It became apparent that analyses of such partial data could only have the status of hypotheses. We could no longer easily convey the impression that our analyses were based on comprehensive evidence inaccessible to teachers. In fact we attempted to increase their access to data in comparison with ours, by suggesting that they should observe each other's classrooms and hold regular feedback sessions with their students.

The strategy embodied a different form of triangulation process to the one we had previously adopted. The previous strategy had involved the collection of data from three points of view: that of the observer, the teacher and the students. But the process was controlled by the observer as was the analysis of the data it generated. The new strategy gave the teacher more control over the collection and analysis of triangulation data.

Our role as outsiders was perhaps more authentically one which facilitated, rather than controlled, teachers' thinking about their practices. The facilitating strategy was articulated as one of formulating diagnostic and action hypotheses for teachers to test in their classrooms. Classroom inquiry became a collaborative process. However, it should be noted that the outsiders' role retained certain controlling elements. The teachers' inquiry was to be focused on hypotheses we generated and these were informed by our theoretical understanding of the pedagogical principles which underpinned the teaching aim.

To that extent teachers' thinking was intentionally (but not necessarily consciously) structured by the outsiders' conceptions of the pedagogical process.

Not all the teachers involved submitted recordings for analysis. The sizeable minority which did so inevitably constituted those who recognized a match between the project's pedagogical perspective and their own. By implication they tended to be the more reflective and self-aware teachers, since self-reflection is an intrinsic dimension of the pedagogical perspective itself. The problem for the central team was now perceived in terms of developing a strategy which would help the majority of participating teachers to implement the principles of procedure in their classrooms.

What I did was to undertake a comparative analysis of the tape transcripts with a view to formulating a set of hypotheses which might be generalized across classrooms and schools. Having formulated the hypotheses, I then transformed them into performance rules. In other words, I created an experimental praxis. The intention was to get the agreement of all teachers to stick to these rules for a stipulated period of time, so that the impact of the action strategies they prescribed could be evaluated. The teachers were asked to collect this impact data and produce evaluation reports at the end of the 'experiment'.

Stenhouse himself was worried about the strategy I had proposed. He felt it was too impositional. His idea was that teachers should change their practices in the light of their own reflection. The choice of pedagogical strategies, he believed, should be theirs. His approach might be illustrated by the following example.

The tapes tended to indicate a prevalent pattern of interaction through which teachers pressurized students to agree with their 'hidden' points of view, thereby failing to realize the principle of 'protecting the expression of divergent views'. The pattern was initiated by such remarks as: 'Do we all agree with what John has just said?' The students' initial response was to remain silent. The teachers then cast an eye around the class until a student said 'Yes'. The discussion was allowed to proceed.

We had asked teachers to test the hypothesis that this pattern had the effect of imposing constraints on the expression of divergent views. If they found that it did, then they were asked to formulate an alternative action strategy for protecting the expression of divergence, and thereby keeping their tendency to constrain such expression in check, e.g. by asking 'Does anyone disagree with what John has just said?'

Stenhouse wanted teachers to generate action – strategies from classroom data. I had gone a step further by formulating the action – strategies for them. Moreover, they were generalized action strategies from a very small sample of classroom practices. My presumption that the strategies reflected a common problem structure for most classrooms caused Stenhouse anxiety. He felt it encouraged a dogmatic and rigid application of general rules rather than a sensitivity to the particular contexts in which teachers needed to realize pedagogical principles. Moreover, Stenhouse feared that my approach would be greeted with hostility, since it would be interpreted as an attempt to prescribe teaching strategies for teachers.

At a conference where we attempted to negotiate the strategies with teachers, it was certainly difficult to get the message across that they were intended as experimental. Some teachers feared we were simply trying to buy them off with rhetoric. The real intent they suspected was an impositional one. Nevertheless, the teachers eventually agreed to shelve their doubts and to do their best to stick to the strategies for a period. Many of them did.

Some of Stenhouse's fears were realized. For example, there was one rule which forbade the provision of anecdotal information in the classroom by students. It was based on data which suggested that ancedotes constrained discussion because there was no way in which the students could contradict the information they contained. Such information was not publicly accessible to critique. The overall effect was to lower the quality of the discourse between students. One teacher had applied this rule with a previous class with remarkable effect on the quality of discussion. But his dogmatic adherence to this rule with another class, subsequent to the agreement we negotiated at the conference, had disastrous consequences. The rule had the reverse effect. It prevented students from saying anything. Upon investigation it transpired that the first class was full of students who had some confidence in their own ideas. The subsequent class was full of students suffering from low self-esteem. The citing of anecdotes was for them a way of approaching discussion without placing their ideas at risk of ridicule from their peers. Stenhouse was right to warn that our strategy could encourage insensitivity to context. Such insensitivity did not simply manifest itself in terms of inappropriate applications of rules in specific contexts. There were teachers who, while applying the rules with some success, never subsequently progressed beyond them. Their teaching strategies did not evolve and develop beyond those prescribed in the rules and became inflexible, rigid and restricted.

Nevertheless some remarkable breakthroughs were achieved by teachers. The approach promoted greater consistency of practice in many classrooms. For example, there was a rule that teachers should not fill up the silent spaces in discussion and thereby remove responsibility from students. Teachers found it incredibly difficult to tolerate silences and tended, after an initial effort, to give in to pressure from students to initiate and sustain the talk. The rule helped many teachers to resist persistent pressure from students to good effect. They suddenly found, after a considerable period of time (weeks rather than days), students accepting greater responsibility for the direction and shape of the discussion.

Many teachers, in a state of intellectual dependency on the diagnostic and prescriptive hypotheses of the central team, began to realize the aspirations of the project in their practices. They adopted strategies which evolved from sources beyond their own understandings of their classroom situation and their role within it. Subsequently some of them produced excellent case studies of their experience of the process of change (See Elliott and MacDonald 1975). In retrospectively trying to explain what happened, teachers' minds were opened to new dimensions of the classroom process. For example, several testified to what appeared to be Damascus-Road-type conversions of students to the value of discussion. After many weeks of facing what appeared to be increasing resistance and hostility towards discussion-based inquiry, the teachers experienced dramatic changes in student behaviour. They began to analyse the causes of such resistance in a very different light, now that they had 'broken through' and experienced success. Their view of students' intellectual capacities shifted and they sought explanations of problems now, not so much in the 'abilities' of their students, as in the forms of social control reproduced through their teaching. The state of dependency we induced, rather than diminishing teachers' capacities for self-reflection, appeared in many cases to have enhanced it.

It seems that one might be able to demarcate two rather different accounts of how teachers reflectively develop their practices. These are:

1   The teacher undertakes research into a practical problem and on this basis changes some aspect of his or her teaching. The development of understanding precedes the decision to change teaching strategies. In other words, reflection initiates action.
2   The teacher changes some aspect of his or her teaching in response to a practical problem and then self-monitors its effectiveness in resolving it. Through the evaluation the teacher's initial understanding of the problem is modified and changed. The decision to adopt a change strategy therefore precedes the development of understanding. Action initiates reflection.

I tend to believe that the first account constitutes a projection of academic bias into the study of teachers' thinking. There is a theory of rational action here in which actions are selected or chosen on the basis of a detached and objective contemplation of the situation. On this theory one can separate out inquiry from practice (taking action). The second account may reflect the natural logic of practical thinking more accurately.

When practical problems arise, the practitioner's first priority is to act quickly in order to resolve it. A request not to change anything pending further inquiry may appear to be a rather time-consuming process when other alternatives are possible. One alternative is to back one's own initial and largely intuitive processing of available data. Another is to draw on the wisdom of other knowledgeable practitioners if one has begun to doubt one's own diagnosis of the situation. In selecting an action strategy on the advice of others, one acts on trust but not non-rationally. It may be more rational to adopt an action strategy on trust initially and then review its merits than to suspend doing something about the situation until all the evidence has been analysed.

While Nero fiddled, Rome burned, and teachers may well feel that, while they do research, the situation disintegrates. When one is faced with a practical problem, it is better to take the calculated risk of getting it wrong, and adjusting one's action strategy retrospectively, than that of not doing anything about the problem until one has fully understood it.

On the second account of practical thinking there is no separation of 'inquiry' and 'practice'. The practice is the form of inquiry: a hypothetical probe into the unknown beyond one's present understanding, to be reviewed in retrospect as a means of extending that understanding. The search for understanding is carried out through changing the practice and not in advance of such changes.

Stenhouse coined the idea of the 'teacher as a researcher' to signify the dependence of pedagogical change on teachers' capacities for reflection. The idea, I believe, is contained in the first account of a reflective practice. The idea of 'educational action research', however, is contained in the second account and more accurately describes the logic of practical thinking underpinning the curriculum reform movement in schools during the 1960s.

The strategy of providing teachers with experimental teaching strategies which I had largely devised marked a critical point in the development of the facilitator's role within the Humanities Project. It marked a transition from the idea of 'teachers as researchers' to the idea of 'teachers as action researchers'. Although the central team prescribed experimental action strategies, it is my belief that many teachers eventually agreed to suspend their own judgement in favour of 'sticking to the rules' because the rules were grounded in evidence of other teachers' classroom practices. Ultimately it was the experience of a small group of peers, represented in the data submitted for analysis, which persuaded teachers to accept the rules on trust for a period. This trust was not blind but informed by evidence, albeit not of the teachers' own practices. Our strategy, in spite of the problems with it, did contain elements which held high potential for enhancing the development of teachers' reflective capacities. The strategy helped to generate a shared body of insights and understandings into the problems of classroom innovation. It did so because teachers were open to evidence of each others' practices and were willing to transcend the limits of their own understanding in learning from it.

The negative element in the strategy lay in the manner in which the experience of classrooms was analysed and disseminated. The hypotheses on which the rules were based were generated entirely by the central team rather than the teachers. For some of the teachers this fact alone was sufficient to generate an uncritical adherence to the rules prescribed, in contrast to a provisional adherence for the sake of experiment. What was required was a strategy which both facilitated the development of shared practical knowledge and freed the practitioners from dependency on the facilitators.

During the dissemination phase of the Humanities Project the central team devised a self-training procedure for teachers (see *The Humanities Curric-ulum Project: An Introduction*, 1970). Teachers were asked to analyse tape recordings of discussions in the light of a series of questions. The questions focused attention on particular patterns of interaction and asked about their effects. For example:

> To what extent do you interrupt students while they are speaking? Why and to what effect?
>
> Do you habitually rephrase and repeat students' contributions? If so, what is the effect of this?

It was suggested that, although they might want to analyse their tapes privately in the first instance, teachers were likely 'to find that, after a certain amount of progress has been made, it is profitable to meet to analyse tapes and discuss developing insights and outstanding problems.'

The procedure was an attempt to support the reflective development of the pedagogy in the context of a self-supporting group of teachers. In most respects it was a revised version of the list of strategies we had asked teachers in the trial periods to test. But it was decided not to make these, or the diagnostic hypotheses on which they rested, explicit. Rather than asking teachers to test diagnostic hypotheses, or experiment with strategies, we asked them to focus on patterns of interaction which the project had found to be problematic in a number of trial-school classrooms. In this way it was hoped that teachers would examine the extent to which such patterns operated in their own practices and then generate hypotheses about their effects, together with possible action strategies for resolving the problems identified. The procedure aspired to help our teachers generate, as well as test, hypotheses for themselves, and to identify those which could be generalized across classrooms.

The problem with this self-training procedure is that the hypotheses and strategies the project team had in mind could easily be inferred from the questions. It is therefore questionable whether the procedure was any more effective in fostering independent reflection amongst teachers than a pro-cedure which made the accumulated practical insights of the project quite explicit. Those in search of prescriptive dogma could easily construct it from the list of questions.

What the project could not avoid, if it aspired to providing real support for teacher development at the dissemination phase, was making accessible to teachers in some form the shared practical knowledge and insights accumu-lated in the initial trial phase. And in doing so there was always a risk that teachers would handle such knowledge dogmatically and uncritically, rather than pro-visionally and experimentally. I am far from convinced that our self-training procedure was more effective in promoting reflective practice than the list of experimental strategies we had negotiated with our trial-school groups of teachers. It could equally be interpreted as the product of 'insights' generated by academic experts on the central team rather than the product of teachers' reflective practices. Having transformed diagnostic and action hypotheses into focused questions, the project team could not then describe the process of hypothesis generation. The procedure tended to reinforce a tendency to assume that the hypotheses implicit in the questions were generated by the experts who asked the questions.

Subsequent to the Humanities Project's official 'life', local education authorities (LEAs) in the United Kingdom (UK) during the 70s used checklists of questions as a key strategy in attempts to get teachers to self-evaluate their practices (see Elliott 1983b). The checklists were largely produced by local inspectors and advisers employed by the LEAs. The strategy, after a few years of immense popularity amongst local officials, was largely dropped during the early 80s. Teachers resisted the checklists because they quickly discerned the rules in them. They interpreted this 'self-evaluation' strategy as part of a general strategy to increase bureaucratic control over the performance of teachers. The checklist syndrome has now reappeared in the context of the development of teacher-appraisal schemes in the UK. This time it is not the teachers who evaluate their practices in the light of prescribed questions, but their super-ordinates in management roles. Again, the origins of the 'knowledge' implicit in the questions and its evidential basis are not made explicit.

Checklists generally appear to be a strategy for controlling how teachers think about practice while trying to disguise that this is what they are. I do not think our 'self-training procedure' escaped this criticism. It obscured the extent to which the implicit hypotheses and action strategies were generated from teachers' own thinking about their classroom practices. I would argue that in the Humanities Project we never satisfactorily resolved the issue of how one facilitates autonomous reflective practice. And this was because we were reluctant to relinquish control over pedagogical theory. Both the list of experimental action strategies and the self-training procedure were structured by the project teams' understanding of pedagogical aims and principles. We did not understand that, in reflecting about their practices, teachers could not only develop their teaching strategies, but also develop their understanding of the aims and principles they sought to realize through them.

However, if we adopt the Aristotelian view that practical inquiry is a form of practical philosophy, because it involves reflecting about practice and the values which constitute its ends in conjunction, then we must enable teachers to develop pedagogical theory as well as pedagogical strategy through reflective practice (Elliott 1983b, 1987). Within the Humanities Project we treated pedagogical theory as our territory and thereby ultimately controlled the extent to which teachers could develop their pedagogy reflectively. The idea of 'teachers as researchers' was bound to a context in which reflection was confined to empirical rather than conceptual inquiry, the latter remaining the territory of specialist theorists.

The attempts of the Humanities Project team to facilitate reflective practice in schools generated an important conceptual distinction between the 'research' role of the outsider in relation to the 'research' role of the insider practitioner. (see Elliott, 1976–7). Stenhouse contrasted the *first-order inquiry* of the teachers with the *second-order inquiry* of the central team. The teachers' inquiry was focused on the problems of developing pedagogical strategies consistent with educational aims and principles. The team's inquiry was focused on the problems of facilitating teachers' reflective capacities. The team members were cast in the role of teacher developers which was also conceptualized as a form of reflective practice. The view of the relationship between external academic change-agents and practitioners within the curriculum-development process went through a transition from the idea of collaborative research into the problems of developing the pedagogy to the idea of each party focusing on a quite distinct domain of practical investigation. The external change agents' second-order inquiry into the problems of facilitating the development of teachers' reflective capacities supports and at times intersects with the first-order pedagogical inquiry of teachers.

This distinction emerged as the project's facilitation strategies moved away from getting teachers to test hypotheses generated by us towards helping teachers to take more responsibility for hypotheses generation themselves. This transformation was itself the product of an increasing reflexive awareness amongst the central team of the hidden forms of control they exercised over teachers' practical thinking. How to facilitate such thinking, without manipulating and distorting it for our own ends, became a major focus for reflection and discussion. Although this was a problem we did not resolve, sufficient progress was made to provide me with an impetus for future deliberation in the context of two action-research projects I was subsequently involved with.

The emergence of a second-order form of practical inquiry engaged in by external facilitators of teacher development has implications for the role of evaluation in curriculum development. The Humanities Project had an evaluation unit as well as a development team. During the funded life of the project this unit also made a contribution to the generation of seminal ideas which were not unconnected with those of the development team.

Stenhouse and his team had articulated a *process model* of curriculum development, in contrast to the *objectives model* in which the quality of teaching was the critical issue rather than the quality of the curriculum materials. The idea of 'teachers as researchers' emerged within this context as an explanatory account of teaching quality. The quality of teaching depended on the development of teachers' reflexive powers.

Stenhouse's process model of curriculum development posed a problem for the evaluation team attached to the project under the leadership of Barry MacDonald (1970). The team could not design an evaluation based on measurements of goal achievement, since the project had refused to specify behavioural objectives as a basis for its work. Moreover, the project had emphasized the importance of particular contexts for the way curriculum practices shaped up. The evaluation team concluded that generalizations about innovations needed to be derived from comparisons of complex case data rather than from aggregated data which abstracted from contexts of practice to provide gross yields on objectives. Psychometric methods were rejected in favour of qualitative methods which identified and described the significant variables operating in particular contexts.

The evaluation team focused on the organizational context of the innovation. It case-studied schools with a view to examining the ways in which organizational climates, policies and structures interacted with pedagogy in classrooms. It also monitored our attempt within the development team to support classroom innovation. The Evaluation Unit published a regular newsletter in which case data was used to portray the project in schools, and the issues, problems and possibilities it raised within them.

MacDonald and his team spearheaded the development of a naturalistic methodology for the evaluation of educational programmes in the UK (See Simons 1987). They also shaped this methodology with an educative intent. The role of the evaluator they argued was to provide information to all those who held a legitimate stake in the programme, e.g. the sponsor, school managers, administration, teachers and the central development team. It is not for the evaluation to judge the programme's merits. Judgement is the preserve of its audiences. The task of evaluation is to assemble and organize data bases which others could use to develop their understanding.

I have described the approach of the evaluation unit in some detail because it is necessary to point out the division of labour which existed amongst project staff. Whereas the development team focused on materials production and implementation problems in classrooms, the evaluation unit focused on the organizational and system context, and the interactions between the development team and teachers. The development team were interventionist and committed to the aims and principles of the project. The evaluation unit took an independent and impartial stance. Moreover, the audience of the central developers largely consisted of teachers, while the evaluation unit reported to multiple audiences, some in positions of power and influence over the future of the programme.

One of the effects of the evaluation was to heighten awareness amongst teachers and the central development team of how the organizational ethos impacted on pedagogy. Attempts to explain problems in realizing the pedagogical principles in practice referred to factors in the organizational and system context which shaped and constrained teachers' and students' interactions. The focus of the teachers' and team's research may have been on classroom events, but this didn't confine the data-collection process to classrooms. In this respect there was a great deal of exchange of information. The evaluation unit not only fed information to teachers and the central developers, but both these parties contributed information to the evaluators.

There is also no doubt in my mind that the emergence of a reflexive attitude amongst the central developers was stimulated by the questions and issues posed by the evaluation unit. However, there is an issue about whether the division of labour between external change agents and evaluators is the best way of organizing support for curriculum development. Certainly a growing tension developed on this issue between Stenhouse and MacDonald subsequent to the Humanities Project. MacDonald argued for the necessity of strong independent evaluations of innovatory programmes. Stenhouse argued that evaluation should not be a specialized role, but integral to reflective practice. This was an issue I had an opportunity to explore in two subsequent projects.

The Ford Teaching Project: educational researchers as teacher educators

The Ford Teaching Project was sponsored by the Ford Foundation from 1973 to 1975. It had a central team of two academics: myself and Clem Adelman. The project involved over 40 teachers in 12 schools undertaking action research into the problems of implementing inquiry/discovery methods in their classrooms. The schools covered the full age-range and the teachers were drawn from different subject areas. My aspiration in designing the project was to explore the possibility of teachers' developing a common stock of professional knowledge about the problems of realizing an alternative to the traditional pedagogy which had so long prevailed in classrooms. This would involve teachers in communicating across some of the long-established boundaries in initial and in-service teacher education, e.g. between the primary and secondary sectors and different subject areas.

The project was a response to a clear problem which had emerged across the curriculum-reform movement in both primary and secondary education. The vast majority of innovatory projects, whether nationally or locally initiated, espoused the use of 'inquiry' or 'discovery' methods in the classroom. External change agencies assumed that, in order to implement such methods, all the teachers required were appropriate curriculum materials. This assumption, as experience with the Humanities Project suggested, proved to be unfounded.

The problems of change at the level of pedagogy needed a more radical analysis than that of 'needing appropriate resource material'. I wanted teachers to make a contribution to this analysis through their own action research. It implies that they should already be committed to using inquiry or discovery methods in their classrooms and to the aims and values implicit in them. The project was not designed as an attempt to convert teachers to an innovatory pedagogy but to support those already committed, but who were nevertheless experiencing difficulty in realizing their aspirations in practice.

In many ways the Ford Project built on foundations laid by the Humanities Project. But it drew on lessons learned from that experience concerning the problems of facilitating pedagogical change. These may be summarized as follows:

- The project was designed as teacher-based action research and not simply as teachers' research. The term 'action research' indicated a clarification of the research paradigm involved, and the relationship between research and teaching. They were not conceived as two separate activities. Teaching was viewed as a form of educational research and the latter as a form of teaching. In other words the two activities were integrated conceptually into a reflective and reflexive practice.
- Teachers were to generate as well as test diagnostic and practical hypotheses.
- Teachers were expected to develop a pedagogical theory as well as explore how to realize it in practice. The approach was to help them to reflect about the aims and values implicit in their definitions of problem situations within the classroom.
- The classroom action research was designed as a co-operative rather than individualistic endeavour aimed at generating shared insights and practices as teachers tested each other's hypotheses in a range of contexts.
- At an early stage the central team defined a second-order action-research role for themselves, aimed at facilitating first-order action research.

The first four of these were clearly reflected in an initial tasks description produced by the central team.

1 To identify and diagnose in particular situations the problems that arise from attempts to implement discovery/inquiry approaches effectively; and to explore the extent to which problems and diagnostic hypotheses can be generalized.
2 To develop and test practical hypotheses about how the teaching problems identified might be resolved, and to explore the extent to which they could be generally applied.
3 To clarify the aims, values and principles implicit in inquiry/discovery approaches by reflecting about the values implicit in the problems identified.

A detailed account of the problems and progress of this project was presented at the 1976 American Educational Research Association (AERA) meeting in San Francisco (see Elliott 1976–7). I do not intend another comprehensive account in this chapter. But in relation to the five features listed above I will briefly attempt to describe and discuss what happened.

As in the Humanities Project, the central team saw itself as collaborating with teachers in the collection and analysis of classroom data. But we were clearer about the inconsistency between enhancing our own expertise and authority as classroom researchers and facilitating reflective practice amongst teachers.

In order to communicate this intent we devised and negotiated an ethical framework with our teachers:

- Individual teachers ought to control both the extent to which, and the conditions under which, other teachers have access to data from their classrooms.
- Headteachers ought to control the extent to which classroom data from their schools is accessible to outsiders, and the conditions under which access is given.
- Individual teachers ought to control the central team's access to both their classrooms and private-interview situations with students.
- Classroom data gathered by the project's central team ought to be made accessible to the teachers concerned, except data over which students have rights of control, i.e. student accounts of classroom problems and teaching strategies.
- Students interviewed by the central team ought to control the extent to which others, including their teachers, have access to their accounts.

This framework was, in fact, designed to reduce the amount of control others, including peers and members of the central team, could exert over teachers' thinking about their practices. It posited others as resources the teachers could use in thinking about their practice without being dependent on their views.

Rather than initiating classroom visits we asked the teacher teams at school level to initiate requests for assistance once they had begun to identify problem areas we might help them to analyse.

During the first few weeks of the project's life very few pedagogical problems were identified by our teachers. In spite of suggestions we had made about techniques and methods of collecting data (teacher and student diary-keeping, teacher–student discussions about classroom processes, tape-recording, case studies) only a few teachers used them initially. Few requests for visits from a central-team member came in. We were faced with a considerable second-order action research problem: how to activate teachers' self-reflection in a manner that was consistent with the ethical framework.

We identified a small number of teachers who appeared to be ready to reflect about their practices in some depth and negotiated access to their classrooms. Although this was a more pro-active intervention than we had originally envisaged, the teachers appeared willing to collaborate and reasonably well motivated. Clem Adelman and I then involved each in a triangulation process. We recorded, either on a tape or a tape/slide, a lesson and interviewed the teacher and a sample of students about it. The interviews were recorded. The triangulation data was then discussed with the teacher, transcribed and circulated, with his or her (and their head teacher's) permission, to all the other teachers in the project. Throughout, the ethical framework was observed. Once the sets of triangulation materials were in circulation around the schools, we generated a list of diagnostic hypotheses for teachers to examine in the light of the data. The schools were organized into local groupings and the teacher teams in them met regularly at the local teachers' centre. The teachers who had participated in the triangulation studies showed a willingness at these meetings to discuss their data openly with peers.

The exercise evoked a great deal of interest amongst the other teachers. One of the major reasons was that it enabled them to compare samples of secondary and primary classroom practice. At the launching conference there had been a great deal of argument about whether primary and secondary practice had anything in common. There was a tendency to place secondary teaching well inside the traditional camp, and primary teaching well inside the progressive camp. Primary-school teachers in particular were amazed about the extent to which the patterns of verbal interaction evidenced in the transcripts appeared to be remarkably similar between primary and secondary classrooms. There was a general tendency to accept our general hypotheses as grounded in the data.

We then asked the teachers to assess the extent to which the hypotheses generalized to their own practices. Many now became very interested in looking at their practices in the light of the hypotheses. Some were unhappy about being involved in a fully blown triangulation exercise which included student feedback, but happy to be observed, or to study recordings of their lessons. We were careful not to prescribe a particular combination of data-gathering techniques, allowing teachers to select whichever techniques they found personally feasible and helpful. Individuals tended to select techniques which provided them with sufficiently illuminating, but not over-threatening, data.

By the second half of the project, after two terms of the project in schools and an interim conference in which teachers shared data, there was a considerable increase of activity. Teachers increasingly observed each other's classrooms, and more requested to be involved in triangulation. About a third of the teachers embarked on case studies of some aspect of their teaching with a particular class. At the final conference a group of teachers undertook the task of distilling a list of general hypotheses about the problems of implementing inquiry/discovery methods from the collective experience. In doing so they not only included those generated by the central team initially. They were able to describe new insights which had emerged from reflection and discussion about classroom experiences during the course of the project. After four terms some teachers had begun to generate, as well as test, hypotheses about life in classrooms.

Although the strategy I have described appeared to be similar in many respects to that employed in the Humanities Project it differed in certain significant respects. First of all, we operated within a code of practice which placed more explicit restrictions on our power to control teachers' thinking about their practice. Secondly, we established an organizational framework of local and central meetings which enabled teachers to reflect together about the triangulation data, and the hypotheses we generated from it, in the presence of the participating teacher. This process made teachers feel less powerless and dependent on the thinking of the central team. In other words, the hypothesis-testing process in the Ford Project was mediated by discourse between peers rather than discourse with the central team. We had established a framework for professional discourse and activated it by generating some initial hypotheses. But we did not mediate this discourse to the same extent as the central team on the Humanities Project. The risk of our controlling its development and outcomes was less. The professional discourse eventually enabled teachers to produce their own hypotheses and to generalize them across classrooms and contexts.

Finally, during the second term of the project, teachers were asked to explicate the theory of teaching implicit in their own classroom practices. As they became aware of the theory which guided their pedagogy they collected and analysed data in the light of their own theory rather than ours. In the Humanities Project it was the facilitators who articulated the theory. Teachers were therefore having to identify and diagnose pedagogical problems in the light of criteria specified by outsiders. Within the Ford Project we tried to help them reflect about their practices in the light of theories they articulated. Under these circumstances one might expect less resistance to gathering and analysing data about classroom processes.

The strategy Clem Adelman and I employed to help teachers articulate their pedagogical theories was as follows. At the initial launching conference we tape-recorded discussions of evidence about classroom practices depicted in transcripts and on videotape. We listened subsequently to the tapes and noted issues which emerged. Many of them revolved around whether or not the practice was an example of inquiry/discovery methods. We had asked teachers to assess the extent to which the practices depicted constituted cases of inquiry or discovery methods. It appeared that disputes about this were grounded in rather different conceptions of such methods.

We extracted from the tapes the terms teachers used to describe the practices they discussed. Amongst the most frequently recurring terms employed were a number of bi-polar pairs. We then interviewed teachers to elicit the meanings they ascribed to these bi-polar constructs. Sometimes teachers, we discovered, used different terms to refer to the same idea, and the same terms to refer to different ideas.

On the basis of the interviews we identified three main dimensions of pedagogical practice which were delineated by the most frequently used terms. These were:

1 *Formal–informal*; *dependent–independent*. The terms *formal–informal* were often used to pick out the degree of intellectual *dependence–independence* of students on the teacher's authority position.
2 *Structured–unstructured*; *subject-centred–child-centred*. *Structure* was

interchangeable with *framework,* but more widely used than the latter. *Structured–unstructured* could be interchanged with *subject-centred– child-centred.* Both these sets of terms referred to the teachers' aims and were used to describe the degree to which they were concerned with getting students to achieve preconceived knowledge outcomes. The more the teacher's aims are concerned with getting preconceived knowledge out- comes, the more structured or subject-centred the teaching; the more they are concerned with the process rather than the products of learning, with how the student is to learn rather than with what, then the more unstructured or child-centred the teaching.

3 *Directed–guided–open-ended.* These three terms picked out points along a single dimension and referred to the methods by which teachers try to implement their aims. The teacher's methods tend to be directive when they prescribe in advance for students how a learning activity is to be performed. They are guided when they are responsive to problems per- ceived by students in performing learning activities, e.g., by asking ques- tions, making suggestions, or introducing ideas in response to task problems cited by students. Open-ended methods are negative in character, being solely concerned with refraining from imposing constraints on students' abilities to direct their own learning. The directed–guided–open-ended dimension picked out the degree of control the teacher tries to exert over the learning activities of the student.

Teachers' accounts of inquiry/discovery teaching were often couched in a combination of terms covering each of these dimensions. We discovered from our analysis of the discussions at the launching-off conference that four different theories of inquiry/discovery were being applied to the data. These were:

1 *Informal-structured-guided.* A teacher can pursue preconceived know- ledge outcomes by guiding students towards them without imposing con- straints on their ability to direct their own learning.
2 *Informal-structured-open-ended.* A teacher can pursue preconceived know- ledge outcomes *and* foster and protect self-directed learning by concentrat- ing solely on removing constraints and refraining from any kind of positive intervention in the learning process.
3 *Informal-unstructured-guided.* A teacher can foster and protect self- directed learning *and* exercise positive influence on the learning process so long as this influence is not exerted to bring about preconceived knowledge outcomes.
4 *Informal-unstructured-open-ended.* A teacher cannot foster and protect self-directed learning *and* pursue preconceived knowledge outcomes *or* exercise positive influence on the learning process. Teaching strategies must be restricted to protecting students' pqwers of self-direction.

During the second term we asked each teacher to identify which theory was implicit in their own practices. During the interim conference at the end of this term we presented teachers with sets of data about each others' practices and asked them to identify the theory implicit in each. By the third term of the project teachers had begun to conclude that informal–structured–guided teaching represented the most commonly held theory of discovery/inquiry teaching. But the data they examined from their own and others' practices suggested that this theory was extremely problematic. Few teachers appeared both to enable independent reasoning and promote the acquisition of pre-specified and sequenced knowledge outcomes. The two processes appeared to be inconsistent with each other. The informal–unstructured–open-ended and informal–structured–open-ended conceptions were also rendered problematic by the study of practice. The former was rendered problematic as a theory of teaching because it appeared to place the teacher in the passive role of not positively intervening to facilitate learning. The latter was rarely manifested but, when it was, appeared to place students in the quite unfair double-bind situation of being expected to know what the teacher wanted without being given any indication of this. Increasingly teachers sought to realize an informal–unstructured–guided pedagogy as one which implied an internally consistent theory. However, it called for the highest level of practical competence on the part of teachers.

The teachers' increasingly active involvement in collecting, sharing and discussing data changed the pedagogical theories underpinning their practices. Indeed such changes tended to result in a growing consensus about how to conceptualize the pedagogy they were striving to implement in the classroom. In the Ford Project teachers developed a pedagogical theory as well as a pedagogical praxis.

In my view the Ford Project not only generated a more emancipated and developed form of reflective practice amongst teachers than the Humanities Project, it also generated a more developed second-order form of reflective practice amongst the external change agents. On the central team we collected and analysed second-order data about our facilitation strategies and their effects on teachers' capacities for self-reflection. The hypotheses (See Elliott 1976–7: 18–21) which emerged tended to focus on the problems of personal change in teachers.

1 **The less teachers' personal identity is an inextricable part of their professional role in the classroom, the greater their ability to tolerate losses in self-esteem that tend to accompany self-monitoring.**

In order to adopt an objective attitude to their practice, teachers need to be able to tolerate the existence of gaps between their aspirations and practice, with a consequent lowering of professional self-esteem. The more teachers self-monitor, the more mastery of their craft appears to elude them. As one teacher commented:

Nothing is ever in a state of stasis, nothing is ever finalized, always there is a reappraisal in the light of new experience. Like children we hanker after the finiteness of things, and like children, we are disturbed when there is frequent reassessment and modification.

Tolerance is difficult to achieve if the sole source of teachers' personal achievement and satisfaction lies in their classroom practice. To tolerate losses of self-esteem, it becomes necessary for them to get satisfaction from their performances in extra-professional situations. We had little success with those teachers whose personal identity was inextricably linked with their professional role in the classroom.

2 **The less financial and status rewards in schools are primarily related to administrative and pastoral roles, the more teachers are able to tolerate temporary losses of self-esteem with respect to classroom practice.**

This is particularly true in our expanding reorganized secondary schools. Systematic reflection on practice takes time, and it was our secondary teachers who complained most about lack of time. Does this situation mean that they work harder than our primary- and middle-school teachers? Not necessarily. For primary-school teachers, the demands of reflecting about the classroom constitute an extension of their existing commitment to the activity of teaching. But secondary-school teachers are increasingly committed to administrative and pastoral functions that are only indirectly connected with the classroom. Thus the demand to give more to the classroom situation generates conflict between alternative commitments.

Almost without exception those teachers with the least capacity for self-criticism have been those who have identified themselves strongly with roles outside the classroom situation. It is as if they can function without severe personal stress in a number of fragmented roles within the system only by maintaining a low degree of self-awareness about their class-room performance. The only way to resolve such stress is either to identify exclusively with the administrative or pastoral roles so that the quality of teaching no longer impinges on questions of self-esteem, or to withdraw from the former and sacrifice status and opportunity completely.

One of the current myths in education is that teaching experience necessarily qualifies a person to make educational policy decisions. Yet given the increasing role fragmentation in educational institutions, it is in fact extremely difficult for a person to move into a policy-making role without sacrificing depth for shallowness of understanding in the class-room. We reached a stage in the project where some of our teachers were faced with the problem of school and department heads who were so out of touch with the reality of the classroom that they were incapable of responding supportively.

3 The more teachers value themselves as action researchers, the greater their ability to tolerate losses of self-esteem.

We found that once teachers began to perceive themselves as action researchers, they developed a greater tolerance of gaps between aspirations and practice. An outside participant observer can do much to help teachers develop this alternative self by treating them as partners in research activities.

4 The more teachers perceive classroom observers as researchers rather than evaluators, the greater their ability to tolerate losses of self-esteem.

For our teachers an 'evaluator' ascribes praise and blame and allows few rights of reply. The 'researcher' role we tried to adopt focused on the practice rather than the practitioner. We tried to set our appraisals of practice in a context of dialogue with the teacher. Within this role teachers tended to perceive us as non-judgemental. Our refusal to ascribe blame helped at least some teachers to tolerate the gaps between aspirations and practice.

5 The more access teachers have to other teachers' classroom problems, the greater their ability to tolerate losses in self-esteem.

Once our teachers began to realize that others had similar problems and were able to study them objectively, they tended to tolerate losses in their own self-esteem more easily.

6 The more teachers are able to tolerate losses in self-esteem, the more open they are to student feedback.

Many of our teachers claimed that student feedback was the most threatening kind of feedback they could have. This is possibly so because students are in the best position to appraise teachers' practice. Openness to student feedback therefore indicates willingness to change one's appraisal of oneself as a practitioner.

7 The more teachers are able to tolerate losses in self-esteem, the more open they are to observer feedback.

Even though not as threatening as student feedback, observer feedback is still threatening enough.

8 The more teachers are able to tolerate losses in self-esteem, the more willing they are to give other teachers access to their classroom problems.

Our experience indicates that initially teachers are more open with professional peers from other schools, especially if they are teaching a different age-range, than with teachers in their own schools. Our inter-disciplinary teams tended to collapse in secondary schools because inter-departmental competition made openness between teachers difficult.

9 The more open teachers are to student feedback the greater their ability to self-monitor their classroom practice.

The reasons for this and the next two hypotheses have been explained in an earlier section.

10 The more open teachers are to observer feedback the greater their ability
    to self-monitor their classroom practice.
11 The more open teachers are to feedback from other teachers, the greater
    their ability to self-monitor their classroom practice.
12 The greater teachers' ability to self-monitor their classroom practice,
    the more they experience conflict between their accountability as edu-
    cators for how students learn (process) and their accountability to
    society for what they learn (in terms of knowledge outcomes).
       Self-monitoring sensitizes teachers to accountability issues. The issues
    presented themselves in the project as a dilemma between protecting
    self-directed learning and pursuing preconceived knowledge outcomes.
13 The more able teachers are at self-monitoring their classroom practice,
    the more likely they are to bring about fundamental changes in it.
       This is the main premise on which the project was founded. Our
    experience tends to confirm it. Once teachers began to clarify and test their
    practical theories, the new theories generated tended to be reflected in
    changes in practice. The main problem is getting teachers to self-monitor
    their practice.

(Elliott 1976–7)

Some of these hypotheses refer to the organizational and system contexts in
which teachers work. The second hypothesis links teachers' capacities for
self-reflection with the distribution of financial and status awards in schools.
The fourth pinpoints the importance of institutional arrangements which
enable teachers to share their experiences of classroom life. The twelfth
hypothesis suggests that reflective practice in schools generates an awareness
of the dilemma between realizing a worthwhile educational process and
meeting the social demand for prespecified learning outcomes, and of the
influence of the institution on the ways they have attempted to reconcile
education with social reproduction.

Reflective practice implies reflexivity: self-awareness. But such an awareness
brings with it insights into the ways in which the self in action is shaped and
constrained by institutional structures. Self-awareness and awareness of the
institutional context of one's work as a teacher are not developed by separate
cognitive processes: reflexive and objective analysis. They are qualities of the
same reflexive process. Reflexive practice necessarily implies both self-
critique and institutional critique. One cannot have one without the other.

This became very clear in the Ford Project. Those who developed their
capacities for action research displayed a considerable critical awareness of the
institutional constraints on the development of their teaching. But they found it
difficult to establish a critical discourse on these matters within the institution
as a whole. Few schools at the time had established organizational forms which
fostered institutional self-critique.

Crucial here were headteachers and others in senior management roles in schools. When we negotiated the project their attitude in most schools was a rather *laissez-faire* one. The participation of teachers in the project, they felt, was up to individuals to decide. If they wanted to be involved, that was fine. But if they didn't, that was fine too. The project was seen as of possible benefit to individual teachers rather than of benefit to the institution as a whole. What transpired in any classroom was the responsibility of the teacher involved, not of the institution. How the latter enabled or constrained quality in teaching was not a question many of the 'managers' appeared to be asking.

The institutional structures which shape teachers' practices in classrooms also shape their thinking about their practices. In many of our schools teachers' opportunities for reflecting about their practices with each other were severely limited. This in turn limited their opportunities for both self and institutional critique.

As the funded life of the Ford Project drew to a close, it became clear that action research would not be maintained, let alone increased, in many of the schools, once the support structures we had established were removed. How to institutionalize action research in schools and the educational system emerged as a major problem for our second-order action research. But it was too late to address that problem in the context of the Ford Project. It was impossible to facilitate institutionalization without continued external funding. The university context of the facilitators themselves did not provide resources for working with teachers collectively inside the system. Resources were only allocated for working with individuals outside the system when they attended academic courses.

Subsequent to the Ford Project the best we could do, with a small grant from the Ford Foundation, was to create a network of teachers and teacher educators who were interested in classroom action research. The project had attracted a great deal of national and some international interest. Other action-research projects had begun to emerge, and some academics, including myself, were attempting to restructure award-bearing in-service courses at diploma and masters levels to support and foster reflective practice in schools (see Elliott, J. 1981a and 1978). The Classroom Action-Research Network (CARN) was established in 1976 to enable individuals and groups committed to action research in the UK and other countries to communicate with each other and share experience through correspondence, papers documenting the experience of action research and conferences. This international network is still flourishing.

In 1981 I embarked on another funded classroom action-research project with teachers. The design of this project embodied a number of strategies which emerged from my thinking about the problems of implementing action research in the Ford Project schools.

The Teacher–Student Interaction and Quality of Learning Project (TIQL)

This piece of action research was funded by the Schools Council from 1981–3 and focused on the problems of 'teaching for understanding' within the context of the public examinations system. It had a team of four part-time and one full-time external facilitators based at the Cambridge Institute of Education. The full-time person was David Ebbutt, an ex-Ford Project teacher.

Bearing the institutionalization problem in mind we selected nine schools in which the senior management was concerned with staff development at the level of the classroom. The way we identified the schools was to locate a number of senior managers who had undertaken classroom action research as part of an award-bearing in-service diploma or masters course at the Cambridge Institute of Education. We then asked each of them to collaborate with us in facilitating teacher-based action research into the problem area for investigation. The facilitation role was divided between internal and external facilitators in schools. We also made it clear to the inside facilitators that they were expected to develop strategies which enabled the institution to support, acknowledge, disseminate and respond to the teachers' action research.

We felt that many of the problems of institutionalizing action research in schools could be fruitfully explored by a person who was both in a power role within the organization and in the role of an action-research facilitator. Any conflict between organizational structures and reflective practice would be manifested in the manager-facilitator's experience and clarified, even resolved, through his or her own second-order action research.

We therefore built into the design of the project an internal management responsibility for second-order action research into the problems of institutionalizing classroom action research. In this way it was hoped that the project would foster both reflective practice at the classroom level and reflective management at the school level. The role of the external team was to facilitate action research at both the level of the classroom and the level of the organization.

With respect to the classroom level we helped individuals to collect and process data about their practices. We responded to requests from the internal facilitators to support particular teachers they had identified as wanting, or in need of, help.

Although we helped teachers to collect and analyse data, we emphasized their ownership of it and their responsibility for disseminating the insights they derived from it. We did not take data out of the school, except on a short-term basis to prepare for a discussion with a teacher. Nor did we disseminate any analyses of data. Instead we organized twice-termly inter-school meetings as a basis on which teachers could share case-study accounts of their practices in relation to particular problems they had identified. We didn't frame their problem definitions by a predetermined pedagogical theory. In fact we resisted attempts by local education inspectors to get the teachers to work to a technical model of teaching in which they prespecified the aim of 'teaching for understanding' into precise learning outcomes. We argued that, as teachers collected data around what they felt to be problems in realizing this aim, they would begin to ask questions about the nature of the aim itself.

By the end of the project teachers had clarified, through reflection and discussion, a list of principles they believed to be implied by the aim. (See Ebbutt, D. and Elliott, J. (eds) 1985 pp. 135–6, 12.1–12.3). Moreover, we were able to feed into this process, at the teachers' request, theoretical literature about the nature of understanding. In this way we helped teachers link their reflections to a wider body of theory without promoting intellectual dependence.

By the end of the project 20 case studies had emerged from action-research in schools (see Elliott and Ebbutt (eds) 1986). Teachers subjected these to a comparative analysis exercise at a final project conference. They grouped the case studies around the major problem areas they had clarified together over the two years of the project. From this analysis a number of diagnostic and action hypotheses were generated in relation to the problem areas. The teachers then grounded these in the case-study evidence. The product was a book written almost entirely by themselves (see Ebbutt and Elliott (eds) 1985).

One of the aims of the TIQL project was to demonstrate the capacity of teachers to generate, test and disseminate a common stock of professional knowledge about classroom processes which raised issues concerning the nature of schools as agents of public policy. In order to demonstrate such a capacity we felt that we had to minimize the extent to which we academics controlled what constituted valid knowledge of the educational process, while providing organizational and methodological frameworks which supported reflective practice in classrooms, the development of shared understandings and their dissemination.

In my view this project was the least power-coercive attempt to facilitate reflective practice in classrooms that I have engaged in. It was the project in which I can most honestly claim that the teachers were largely responsible for generating, developing and publicly disseminating understandings of the pedagogical process. They also demonstrated that, given opportunities within their institution for reflection, they were able to articulate and develop the pedagogical theories implicit in their practices.

However, although the idea of building the project around internal facilitators, occupying senior management positions, but committed and competent action researchers, ensured in most schools a measure of institutional support during the project, this was not maintained after the project terminated. It was as if the internal facilitators required their strategies within schools to be validated by a strong external support team possessing influential sponsorship. They had begun to feel isolated and alienated from other managers in the school. Retrospectively we realized that, as with teachers, we needed to work with managers collectively.

This leads me to conclude this chapter with a brief reflection about the relationship between independent evaluations of educational-change pro- grammes and the practitioners, managers and external facilitators of change. MacDonald's naturalistic paradigm of Democratic Evaluation, referred to earlier (see also MacDonald 1974), can be viewed as a set of strategies for facilitating reflective judgements, decisions and actions by all constituent parties whose activities shape and impinge upon processes of teaching and learning. In facilitating reflective practices amongst classroom teachers, one must also facilitate reflective practices amongst school managers, officials in the educational system and the consumers of schooling: students and parents. One cannot realistically foster teachers' learning through action research without also fostering the learning of other parties through this process. Moreover it is clear that this holistic facilitator must have a sphere of independent operation.

The democratic evaluator who collects, organizes and disseminates data from a variety of souces does so as a means of creating an informed and educative discourse which accommodates the views and perspectives of a variety of constituents. The evaluator too is an educator but not just a teacher educator. Stenhouse was right to see evaluation as an integral element of educational practice. But he was wrong to assume that independent evaluators are not themselves engaged in a form of educational practice. The more holistic the approach of the action-research facilitator, the more (s)he will closely resemble the democratic and naturalistic evaluator.

Part II

Action research: dilemmas and innovations

3

The theory–practice problem

Teachers often feel threatened by 'theory'. This chapter examines those
feelings and shows how action research resolves the theory–practice issue.
However, the author argues that action research as a 'cultural innovation' is
inevitably threatening to the traditional professional cultures of both teachers
and academic teacher educators. As a form of mutual professional learning it
requires a transformation of both school and academic cultures.

'Insider' curriculum evaluation and research can be viewed as a resolution of
the theory–practice problem. Some would argue that this is a theoretical
problem in itself: there being many different theories of the relation between
theory and practice. I would argue that first and foremost it is a practical
problem. Let's look at it, not so much from the standpoint of the educational
theorist in academe but 'through the eyes' of practising teachers. From their
point of view theory is something they cannot apply or use in relation to their
practice. Not that this experience as such constitutes a practical problem for
them. They might simply disregard theory as 'useless'. No problem. But I would
suggest the theory–practice relation does constitute a practical problem for
teachers because they feel threatened in some sense by theory. So let's unpack
this experience of threat.

First, teachers feel 'theory' is threatening because it is produced by a group
of outsiders who claim to be experts at generating valid knowledge about
educational practices. This claim to expertise is only too evident in the battery
of procedures, methods and techniques such 'researchers' employ to collect
and process information about insiders' practices. They possess little resemb-
lance to the way teachers process information as a basis for their practical
judgements. Whether the techniques generate psychometric measures,

ethnographies or grounded theories does not matter. They are all symbolic of the power of the researcher to define valid knowledge. Theory for teachers is simply the product of power exercised through the mastery of a specialized body of techniques. It negates their professional culture which defines teaching competence as a matter of intuitive craft knowledge, tacitly acquired through experience. Phenomenologically speaking, from the perspective of teachers, 'theory' is what outside researchers say about their practices after they have applied their special techniques of information processing. As such it is remote from their practical experience of the way things are. To bow to a 'theory' is to deny the validity of one's own experience-based professional craft knowledge.

Second, the feelings of threat may be enhanced if the knowledge generated is couched in the form of generalizations about teachers' practices. If it applies to all contexts of practice, then it implies that the experience of teachers operating in particular circumstances is not an adequate basis on which to generate professional knowledge: this contradicts their own self-understanding. Generalization constitutes the denial of the individual practitioners' everyday experience. It reinforces the powerlessness of teachers to define what is to count as knowledge about their practices. The more the researchers' claim is to generalizable knowledge, the more threatening it is to teachers because it will contradict their experience of themselves as sources of expert knowledge. Teachers will tend to view generalizable knowledge claims as more theoretical than, say, case studies of their practices precisely because they experience them as disconnected from their own experience; although one must not forget that researchers often produce studies of cases to describe and illustrate the general properties of a class of practices, e.g. formal methods of teaching.

Third, feelings of threat are further enhanced by the researchers' employment of models of practice derived from some ideal of society or the human individual. We only have to look at the way in which educational researchers have generated a 'theory of the hidden curriculum' to understand how these idealized models of practice structure the construction of educational knowledge, e.g. such a theory may assert that the curriculum:

- Reproduces the social inequalities and injustices which prevail in society.
- Reinforces passive and dependent thinking and inhibits critical thinking.
- Fosters narrow and limited conceptions of human potentials and abilities, thereby undermining students' self-esteem and restricting personal development.
- Disconnects the acquisition of knowledge from the development of capacities for judgement and discrimination in the complex affairs of everyday life.

These generalizations are not simply threatening because they cite regularities which individual teachers have no control over. Many teachers would acknowledge that their practices are shaped to a degree by factors beyond their control. What is also threatening is that they imply a negative evaluation of teachers: a failure to live up to an ideal model of practice. They place teachers in what Ronald Lang called 'the double-bind situation' where a person is blamed for doing certain things, but given no indication of what (s)he could have done in the circumstances to have avoided blame. Generalizations of the kind cited tend to ignore the contingencies operating in particular practical settings, and provide no indication of how progress in realizing the ideal might be accomplished *in situ*.

The more explicitly an ideal of practice is manifested in a research generalization, the more threatened teachers will be by the researcher's claim to knowledge, and the greater the likelihood that it will be rejected as theoretical, i.e. remote from the teacher's understanding of the realities of life in classrooms.

It is not the suggestion that practice ought to realize human ideals which merits the label 'theory', but the implication that teachers are necessarily to blame for any mismatches. Faced with such an implication, teachers have little choice but to reject the suggestion as 'theory', i.e. as remote from their practical knowledge of the contingencies of life in classrooms. The perceived gap between theory and practice originates not so much from demonstrable mismatches between ideal and practice but from the experience of being held accountable for them.

The 'theory' construct has two major components for teachers. First, it implies 'remoteness' from their professional knowledge/experience. Second, it implies a threat to their professional knowledge and status from the academic community. It is this second component, which, together with the first, renders the theory—practice relation a very real practical problem for teachers. However, there is a sense in which 'the problem' is a convenient one. If 'theory' and 'research' are remote from practice, divorced from its realities, then knowledge about practice remains a private affair. Although somewhat threatening, 'theory' and 'research' also protect teachers' practices as individual realms of private, esoteric, intuitive craft knowledge.

One of the interesting things about the school-based action-research movement is that it has been led and sustained by academic teacher educators operating from the higher-education sector. From time to time 'collaborating' teachers have felt frustrated about the continuing dependence of the movement on academic leadership, but the mini-rebellions from the grassroots have so far not developed into a revolution. It is easy to interpret this as a new form of academic hegemony, and indeed there is an element of truth in such an interpretation. But I also believe that dependence is based on the need for a counter-culture to the traditional craft culture in schools. The values which underpin the traditional craft culture in schools are threatened by the new concept of professionalism embodied in the action-research movement. Indeed I shall argue that the action-research movement constitutes an attempt to transform the traditional professional culture, and will therefore be opposed by its 'guardians'. Teacher-researchers in schools are dependent in their attempts to transform the traditional craft culture on those temporary cultures which evolve in the context of 'projects' and 'courses' led by academics.

The action-research movement in education is as indicative of a transformational tendency in the academic culture of professional training faculties within higher education institutions as of a transformation in the professional culture of teachers.

The major problem any cultural innovation 'from within' faces is the failure of the innovators to free themselves from the fundamental beliefs and values embedded in the culture they want to change. Cultural innovations often fail to realize their radical possibilities by carrying forward too many of the basic assumptions of 'the old order'. Teacher-researchers will be tempted to accommodate themselves to the norms of the professional craft culture. In order to resist such a temptation they will look to higher-education institutions for intellectual, emotional and practical support. But since 'innovatory' teacher educators and educational researchers in these institutions will not be entirely emancipated from the framework of assumptions and values which defined their traditional academic roles as purveyors and generators of theory, there is a very real danger that teachers' attempts to redefine their professionalism through action research will ensnare them in the 'epistemological hegemony' of academe which the traditional craft culture so fiercely resisted. This book explores the problems of transforming the professional culture of teachers into one which supports professional learning through action research.

4
The fundamental characteristics of action research

This chapter systematically explores the key characteristics of action research and shows how it unifies activities often regarded as quite distinct. The author shows how such activities as teaching, educational research, curriculum development and evaluation are all integral aspects of an action-research process.

The author shows how the treatment of different activities as quite disparate functions is a feature of the increasing growth of technocratic systems of surveillance and control in the guise of curriculum reform. However, he argues that this growth generates and stimulates the emergence of an oppositional professional culture in the form of action research. But action research is not simply a reactionary and defensive response to technocratically controlled change. It constitutes a form of creative resistance because it transforms rather than simply preserves the old professional craft culture of teachers.

The fundamental aim of action research is to improve practice rather than to produce knowledge. The production and utilization of knowledge is subordinate to, and conditioned by, this fundamental aim.

The improvement of a practice consists of realizing those values which constitute its ends, e.g. 'justice' for legal practice, 'patient care' for medicine, 'preserving the peace' for policing, 'education' for teaching. Such ends are not simply manifested in the outcomes of a practice. They are also manifested as intrinsic qualities of the practices themselves. For example, if the teaching process is to influence the development of students' intellectual powers in relation to curriculum content, then it must manifest such qualities as 'openness to their questions, ideas, and ways of thinking', 'commitment to free and open discussion', 'respect for evidence', 'a concern to foster independent thinking' and 'an interest in the subject matter'. Teaching mediates students' access to the curriculum and the quality of this mediating process is not insignificant for the quality of learning.

What makes teaching an educational practice is not simply the quality of its educational outcomes, but the manifestation within the practice itself of certain qualties which constitute it as an *educational process* capable of fostering *educational outcomes* in terms of student learning. The concept of education as an end of teaching, as with concepts of the ends of other social practices, transcends the familiar distinction between process and product. Improving practice involves jointly considering the quality of both outcomes and processes. Neither consideration in isolation is sufficient. The quality of learning outcomes is only at best an indirect indicator of the possible quality of the teaching process. The quality of learning outcomes depends on more than the quality of teaching. Whether poor-quality learning outcomes are due to poor teaching is a matter to be determined in particular cases. One cannot simply presume a direct causal relationship. Although assessments of the educational quality of learning outcomes can help teachers reflect about the quality of their teaching, they are insufficient as a basis for evaluating/appraising it. The practice of teaching also needs to be appraised in terms of its intrinsic qualities. Both product and process need to be jointly considered when attempting to improve practice. Processes need to be considered in the light of the quality of learning outcomes and vice versa.

This kind of joint reflection about the relationship in particular circumstances between processes and products is a central characteristic of what Schon has called *reflective practice* and others, including myself, have termed *action research*.

Improving practice, when viewed as the realization of the values which define its ends into concrete forms of action, necessarily involves a continuing process of reflection on the part of practitioners. This is partly because what constitutes an appropriate realization of value is very context bound. It has to be judged afresh in particular circumstances. General rules are guides to reflection distilled from experience and not substitutes for it. What constitutes an appropriate realization of value is ultimately a matter of personal judgement in particular circumstances. But since personal judgements are in principle infinitely contestable practitioners who sincerely want to improve their practices are also under an obligation to reflect continuously about them *in situ*. Values are infinitely open to reinterpretation through reflective practice; they cannot be defined in terms of fixed and unchanging benchmarks against which to measure improvements in practice. The reflective practitioner's understanding of the values (s)he attempts to realize in practice are continually transformed in the process of reflecting about such attempts. Values constitute ever receding standards.

I will now explore the nature of this continuing process of reflection in greater detail. Following the publication of Donald Schon's books on the 'reflective practitioner' (1983 and 1987), the phrase 'reflective practice' has become very fashionable in the discourse of professional development. But there are different kinds of practical reflection which assume different conceptions of the sorts of ends to be practically realized. The educational action-research movement which emerged in the UK twenty years ago did so in opposition to the development of a curriculum technology which stressed the prespecification of measurable learning outcomes (Stenhouse 1975: Chapters 5–7). The movement asserted the importance of process values as a basis for constructing the curriculum. I wish to locate action research in the kind of reflective practice which aims to improve the realization of process values.

When values define the ends of a practice, such ends should not be viewed as concrete objectives or targets which can be perfectly realized at some future point in time. As such they would constitute technical ends which can be clearly specified in advance of practice. Inasmuch as reflection is involved, it constitutes technical reasoning about how to bring about a prespecified end-product. Values as ends cannot be clearly defined independently of and prior to practice. In this context the practice itself constitutes an interpretation of its ends in a particular practical situation. The ends are defined in the practice and not in advance of it.

The kind of reflection involved here is quite different to technical means–ends reasoning. It is both ethical and philosophical. Inasmuch as the reflection is about choosing a course of action in a particular set of circumstances, to realize one's values, it is ethical in character. But since ethical choice implies an interpretation of the values to be realized, reflection about means cannot be separated from reflection about ends. Ethical reflection has a philosophical dimension.

Reflection directed towards the realization of values might be described as practical philosophy (see Elliott 1987). Such a description directs our attention to the role reflective critiques of the value interpretations embedded in practice can play in improving it. Such philosophical critiques enable practitioners to continuously reconstruct their concepts of value in ways which progressively illuminate practical problems and possibilities. Philosophy is not simply an academic discipline dissociated from the realities of everyday social practices and engaged in by specialists operating outside them.

Action research is an alternative way of describing the sort of ethical reflection outlined. In contrast to 'practical philosophy' the term directs attention to the importance of empirical data as a basis for reflectively improving practices. However, this is simply a matter of emphasis in different communicative contexts. Within an ethical practice the quality of reflection about the ends-in-view embedded in it depends on the quality of the data one gathers about it. However, philosophical reflection of this kind itself modifies conceptions of ends in ways which change one's understanding of what constitutes good data about practice. So one cannot improve the methodology of action research independently of philosophical reflection. The two descriptions pick out intersecting and mutually dependent dimensions of ethical reflection about practice. Both descriptions carry an implicit criticism of the tendency to dissociate both philosophy and research from the realities of practice. In relocating them within the practical domain of 'insiders', they constitute part of an attempt to articulate an account of ethical reflection which can defend this domain against the incursion of technical rationality into the way people think about practice. If practical reflection is solely construed as a form of technical or instrumental reasoning, then there is little room not only for philosophical self-reflection about values, but also for the ethical dimension of social practices. The ethical is projected into a realm of ends which can be defined independently of and prior to practice.

In the field of education the term 'action research' was used by some educational researchers in the UK to articulate an alternative paradigm of educational inquiry which supported ethical reflection within the domain of practice. The established positivist paradigm was rejected by these researchers on the grounds that it served the interests of those who looked to research as a source of technical means–ends rules for controlling and shaping the practices of teachers. However, there are signs that action research has become hijacked in the service of technical rationality. Teachers are being encouraged to view action research as an inquiry into how to control pupil learning to produce predefined curriculum objectives or targets without any consideration of the ethical dimension of teaching and learning. I am anticipating that action research will become highly recommended as a strategy for helping teachers to maximize pupils' achievements of national curriculum targets.

The time may have arrived for facilitators of reflective practice to stop using the term 'action research'. I find myself trying to express the idea which it referred to in different words. I have started talking about reflective practice as a 'moral science' (see Elliott 1989a).

Action research improves practice by developing the practitioner's capacity for discrimination and judgement in particular, complex, human situations. It unifies inquiry, the improvement of performance and the development of persons in their professional role. With respect to the latter it informs professional judgement and thereby develops pratical wisdom, i.e. the capacity to discern the right course of action when confronted with particular, complex and problematic states of affairs. I know of no better statement about the nature of practical wisdom than the prayer of St Francis where he asks God for the patience to accept the things he cannot change, the courage to change what is in his power to change and the wisdom to know the difference. If action research consists in the development of this form of practical understanding, it constitutes a form of inquiry which fully acknowledges the 'realities' which face practitioners in all their concreteness and messy complexity. It resists the temptation to simplify cases by theoretical abstraction but will use and even generate theory to illuminate practically significant aspects of the case. In action research analytic or theoretical understanding has a subordinate relation to the development of a synthetic or holistic appreciation of the situation as a whole.

Action research therefore constitutes a resolution to the theory–practice issue as it is perceived by teachers. Within this form of educational inquiry, theoretical abstraction plays a subordinate role in the development of a practical wisdom grounded in reflective experiences of concrete cases. Although theoretical analysis is an aspect of reflective experience, its subordination to practical understanding and judgement ensures that it does not become dissociated from the realities which confront practitioners. It is no longer perceived as 'remote'. However, does its threatening character disappear because it is controlled by the search for practical understanding? I shall argue later that, for those teachers who are anxious to maintain the traditional craft culture in schools, action research is even more threatening than traditional outsider research.

Practical wisdom as the form of the practitioner's professional knowledge is not stored in the mind as sets of theoretical propositions, but as a reflectively processed repertoire of cases. Theoretical understandings are encapsulated in such cases, but it is the latter which are primarily utilized in attempts to understand current circumstances. Comparisons with past cases illuminate practically relevant features of the present situation. Inasmuch as such comparisons prove insufficient in furnishing a practically relevant understanding of a situation, some explicit theoretical analysis will be appropriate, and the insights which emerge will inform and underpin the subsequently stored narrative description of the case.

A felt need, on the part of practitioners to initiate change, to innovate, is a necessary precondition of action research. It is the feeling that some aspect(s) of a practice need to be changed if its aims and values are to be more fully realized, which activates this form of inquiry and reflection. I have argued earlier, in Chapter 1, that educational action research in the UK emerged in a context where teachers became dissatisfied with traditional curriculum provision and were beginning to initiate radical changes in both curriculum content and the processes whereby it was constructed and mediated to students in schools. Action research, at least in embryo, emerged as a form of curriculum development in innovatory schools during the 60s. All academics, like Stenhouse and me, did was to begin to discern and articulate its underlying logic. I believe this to be an important task for academic educationalists to perform, but it is one which is parasitic on teachers' attempts reflectively to change their curricular and pedagogical practices in schools. In articulating the logic of inquiry implicit in such attempts, the academic educationalist can help to nurture, protect and sustain an emerging professional culture in the face of powerful conservative and technocratic forces operating within the educational system and the wider society.

Action research unifies processes often regarded as quite disparate, e.g.

teaching, curriculum development, evaluation, educational research and professional development. First, teaching is conceived as a form of research aimed
at understanding how to translate educational values into concrete forms of
practice. In teaching, diagnostic judgements about practical problems and
action hypotheses about strategies for resolving them are reflectively tested
and evaluated. Second, since it is action hypotheses about how to translate
values into practice which are being tested, one cannot separate the research
process of testing hypotheses from the process of evaluating teaching. Evaluation is an integral component of action research. Third, curriculum development is not a process which occurs prior to teaching. The development of
curriculum programmes occurs through the reflective practice of teaching.
The improvement of teaching is not so much a matter of getting better at
implementing an externally designed curriculum, but of developing one;
whether it be self-initiated or initiated by outsiders.

Curriculum programmes may be viewed as sets of action hypotheses about
how to mediate curriculum content to learners in an educationally worthwhile manner. Such hypotheses are continuously tested and reconstructed in
the practice of teaching through action research. From an action-research
perspective, the improvement of teaching and the development of the teacher
are integral dimensions of curriculum development. Hence the saying that
'there can be no curriculum development without teacher development'. It is
not implying that teachers have to be developed before curricula can be
properly implemented, e.g. by attending in-service courses. Rather it implies
that curriculum development in itself constitutes a process of teacher
development.

Action research integrates teaching and teacher development, curriculum
development and evaluation, research and philosophical reflection, into a
unified conception of a reflective educational practice. This unified conception
has power implications inasmuch as it negates a rigid division of labour in
which specialized tasks and roles are distributed across hierarchically organized activities. A unified educational practice empowers 'insiders', i.e. teachers.
Inasmuch as outsiders' specialized tasks and roles can be justified, their aim
must be to support and facilitate reflective educational practice without
destroying the unity of its constituent parts. This can happen only if the more
specialized activities have the subordinate function of nurturing the unity of
reflective practice as opposed to imposing on practitioners a hegemony of
specialist expertise with the function of externally regulating their activities.

Action research does not empower teachers as a collection of autonomously
functioning individuals reflecting in isolation from each other. The practice of
teaching is not simply the creation of individuals in institutional settings. It is
shaped by structures which transcend the power of any single individual to
effect change. This structuration is manifest in the selection, sequencing and
organization of curriculum content; in the programmes of learning tasks which
govern how that content is handled; in the ways pupils are socially organized,

and time and resources are allocated and distributed, in relation to learning tasks. All of these structural dimensions shape teachers' practices and therefore circumscribe the kinds of curricular experiences they offer pupils.

Teachers' attempts through action research to improve the educational quality of pupils' learning experiences necessitates reflection about the ways in which curriculum structures shape pedagogy. 'Educational' action research implies the study of curriculum structures, not from a position of detachment, but from one of a commitment to effect worthwhile change.

Teacher researchers who neglect the operation of curriculum structures reduce action research to a form of technical rationality aimed at improving their technical skills. This is most likely to happen when teachers reflect in isolation from each other. The isolated individual who addressed the way curriculum structures shaped his/her practice would become aware of his powerlessness to effect change. For the isolated teacher ignorance is bliss. It allows such a teacher to sleep at night by living under the illusion that the improvement of practice is largely a matter of developing technical skills. What the teacher will fail to recognize is that the illusion is itself a product of the operation of powerful structures on the practice of isolated practitioners. Not only does it mask their powerlessness, but it also compensates them with a narrowly circumscribed sense of power: namely, to effect technical improvements in their practice. In these circumstances teachers will dissociate their professional development from curriculum development and evaluation/ research, and thereby allow others to utilize such activities as forms of hierarchical surveillance and control over their practices.

The emergence of hierarchalized, specialist functions to control and regulate primary practice is a characteristic of highly centralized and technocratic systems of schooling. The recent rapid growth of such a system in England and Wales might be explained in terms of the special vulnerability of the traditional craft culture which thrived in the previously decentralized system. This culture largely supported a non-reflective, intuitive and highly routinized form of practice which was executed in the private world of the classroom in isolation from professional peers. The growth of a technocratic system of surveillance and control over practice is a difficult thing for members of an individualized and esoteric craft culture to resist. One form of resistance is simply to engage in various kinds of oppositional conduct to protect the sense of esoteric expertise embedded in the culture. It is a 'no change' protectionist scenario which elicits little support from pupils, parents and the general public. In the absence of such support the oppositional conduct legitimates the very thing it was intended to resist; namely, a technocratic system of hierarchical surveillance and control over teachers' practices. Resistance based on professional conservatism and protectionism is on a hiding to nothing.

However, there is another form of resistance which is creative rather than being simply oppositional. It involves the transformation of the professional culture into one which supports collaborative reflection about practice and takes the experiences and perceptions of clients (pupils, parents, employers) into account in the process. When teachers engage in collaborative reflection on the basis of common concerns and involve their clients in the process, they develop the courage to critique the curriculum structures which shape their practices, and the power to negotiate change within the system which maintains them. The system needs teachers' co-operation, and large-scale professional disenchantment calls for negotiated compromise.

I would argue that the widespread emergence of collaborative action research as a teacher-based form of curriculum evaluation and development is a creative response to the growth of technical-rational systems of hierarchical surveillance and control over teachers' professional practices. Out of the still smouldering embers of the traditional craft culture the phoenix of a collaborative reflective practice arises to offer creative resistance to the hegemony of the technocrat. As it does so, however, it confronts aspiring reflective practitioners with a number of dilemmas which I shall now describe. In doing so I will identify various temptations they will need to overcome if the dilemmas are to be resolved.

5

The dilemmas and temptations of the reflective practitioner

The chapter analyses in some detail the major dilemmas teacher researchers have experienced in attempting to carry out research in their schools. The author attempts to clarify the kinds of 'resolutions' which are unhelpful because they reinforce the status quo within the traditional teacher culture. He points out the ways the dilemmas of teacher researchers would need to be resolved if 'insider research' in schools is to play a transformative role with respect to the professional culture.

Simons (1985) argues that the popularity of school self-evaluation 'indicates its susceptibility to differing ideological dispositions'. Her own disposition is to favour a process not unlike the kind of collaborative action research I have described. She defines it as a process which embodies the values of openness, shared critical responsibility and rational autonomy, and argues that they clash with the primary values which appear to regulate life in schools; namely: privacy, territory and hierarchy. Simons appears to be describing central aspects of the traditional craft culture, although 'authority' might be preferable in this context to 'expertise'. Hierarchies can transmit power without authority, inasmuch as the latter implies the legitimate use of power in the eyes of subordinates. Within the traditional craft culture of teaching, authority is ascribed on the basis of 'experience' and 'expertise' as a teacher of children. Headteachers who are inexperienced or incompetent, when it comes to handling children, carry little authority with their teachers.

Dilemmas for 'insider researchers' can arise from a clash of professional values between those which underpin the traditional craft culture and those which underpin an emergent culture of reflective practice. This clash occurs not so much between as within individuals. A situation in which a group of teachers unambiguously embraces the values of reflective practice and as a result is opposed by others who unambiguously embrace the values of the craft culture, constitutes a problem for both groups but a dilemma for neither. Dilemmas arise when individuals experience the clash of cultures within. They may not be consciously aware of these internal contradictions, in which case dilemmas can manifest themselves as interpersonal conflicts in which each party projects one of the clashing sets of values on to the other and thereby 'disowns' it. This enables the members of one group to view themselves as an enlightened élite and of the other to cast themselves as the guardians of common sense. It is not a very productive state of affairs with respect to any radical transformation in the professional culture of teachers more generally. The propagation of exclusive élites in institutional pockets is no answer to the problem of reconstructing teachers' professionalism.

Any such reconstruction must be grounded in the meta-reflections of insider researchers about the dilemmas they face in doing action research in schools. Inasmuch as some of these dilemmas are constituted by the values of the traditional craft culture, we could attempt a preliminary analysis of dilemmas in terms of the issues they raise about the values of 'authority', 'privacy' and 'territoriality'.

Simons (1978) and Elliott *et al.* (1979) formulated hypotheses about problems of insider research in schools following courses they mounted to support and facilitate such activity. James and Ebbutt (1980) have written about the problems they experienced as insider researchers prior to becoming university-based researchers. I have revisited the three papers in an attempt to do a dilemma analysis (see Winter 1982) of the problems they cite. I present this analysis in the hope that it will stimulate and assist the kind of meta-reflection which it is so essential for insider researchers/evaluators in schools to engage in.

Dilemmas

1 Encouraging pupils to critique one's professional practice

Teacher researchers might assume that such an activity affects them only as they operate in the confines of their own classroom. This assumption is based on a shared understanding embedded in the traditional craft culture: namely, 'what I do in my classroom is my business and what you do in yours is your business.' Eliciting critiques from pupils challenges this understanding which teacher researchers/evaluators share with their colleagues, as James and Ebbutt vividly illustrate:

> In a long discussion with someone who was both a colleague and a friend, MJ was charged with undermining her own professional status and, by implication, the professional status of colleagues. By looking at

her own practice in such an explicit way, was she not publicly confessing to shortcomings in her expertise, and was this not likely to lower the image of the profession? On another occasion her practice of interviewing pupils to obtain feedback on her own lessons in one area of the curriculum, had apparently encouraged pupils to volunteer criticism to other teachers who were unprepared for such a response, whether it be negative or otherwise.

The dilemma here for the teacher researcher arises from a conflict between the value of critical openness to pupils and respect for the professional expertise of colleagues and their right to exercise authority within the confines of their own classroom. There are a number of ways in which a teacher researcher might be tempted to resolve this dilemma. They may cease in their attempts to elicit pupil critiques altogether or to impose certain limits on both the content and form of such critiques, e.g. 'Please do not compare these lessons with other teachers' lessons', 'Do not mention other teachers by name', 'Do not talk about specific lessons, including mine, or about specific teachers, including me. Just talk generally about the sort of lessons you like and don't like, and why?' Temptations to suppress, restrict or structure the critiques of pupils tacitly communicates a protectionist and conservative message: namely, that the exercise of authority should be questioned only under the terms and conditions established amongst the authorities themselves.

James and Ebbutt suggest an alternative way out of the dilemma. They decided to 'let colleagues . . . know what we are doing, and why' in an attempt to create a supportive environment for insider research in their schools. Instead of compromising with the prevailing view of professionalism, they continued to elicit pupil critiques while embarking simultaneously on a series of conversations with colleagues about the professional purposes such critiques might serve.

2 Gathering data

While data about parental perceptions is commensurate with the action researcher's commitment to critical openness, it is, like pupil data, incommensurate with the conception of professional authority embedded in the traditional craft culture. Moreover, it is within this particular client domain that the hierarchical structure of traditional authority is brought into play through the role of the headteacher. James and Ebbutt argue that the head is as much of a gatekeeper when it comes to insider researchers' access to parental data as (s)he is to outsider researchers' access. In fact, I would tend to argue that the heads' power with respect to the former is far greater than it is with the latter. For outsider researchers to believe that it is not, is a considerable testimony to the extent to which they were previously socialized into the traditional norms of the professional teacher culture. Evidence of such socialization is surely manifest in James and Ebbutt's account of the way in which James depended on her headteacher's permission to secure access to data about parental views. Although permission was eventually granted, it need not have been. The act of seeking permission is itself indicative of a dilemma between respect for the hierarchical structure of professional authority and the value of critical openness.

> MJ wanted to find out about the views of parents and rightly anticipated the head's concern to know, if not control, all communication with the world outside the school. Thus he was consulted at an early stage and having secured his clearance of the questionnaire no further resistance was encountered.

One might ask: 'What alternatives were open to her?' Would it be unprofessional for a teacher with a specific responsibility in an area of the curriculum to elicit parental views about practice in that area without seeking the head's permission? To do so without making every attempt to involve the head in discussions about the kind of data to collect, how to collect and analyse it, and how to report it and to whom, would clearly undermine his/her role as the professional leader of the staff. But this leadership role need not entail the professional protectionism that seeking permission to elicit parental views implies. The head who sees his/her role as facilitating reflective practice would value the critical openness implicit in teachers' attempts to elicit parental views and support such attempts with positive guidance and help.

Now I am not naïve enough to believe that headteachers generally have the vision, courage and social skills which characterize the qualities of leadership in reflective professional communities. Insider researchers must expect the hierarchy to resist giving up control over its access to certain kinds of data. They may find it extremely difficult to exercise their right of access, in spite of numerous attempts to justify this right professionally in terms of the reflective development of practice. Insider researchers will often need to adopt a developmental perspective, develop patience and avoid the kind of confrontation which musters the forces of reaction within the professional culture. But none of this need involve the kind of trade off which seeking permission from the hierarchy involves. Even if such a trade off can be justified as a pragmatic strategy on a temporary basis, this does not warrant treating it as a methodological principle of insider research. Teacher researchers may not have control over access to all the data they need, but they do not have to succumb to the temptation of methodologically legitimating the gatekeeping activities of professional authorities, thereby allowing the premises of the traditional craft culture to define their professionalism as teachers.

3 Sharing data with professional peers, both inside and outside the school

Such data-sharing promotes a reflective conversation and is at the heart of any transformation of the professional culture. But it carries the risk of bringing latent conflicts and tensions out into the open. Problematic areas of practice become exposed, and the practitioners operating in them become vulnerable to punitive attitudes expressed by self-styled experts who promote this image of themselves by pointing the finger at others. It has been my experience that teacher researchers find sharing data with peers from other schools more conducive to a reflective conversation than sharing it with colleagues. In the former context there are fewer latent conflicts and tensions to be exposed. Teacher researchers may find themselves in a dilemma about risking such exposure even when they feel confident in their ability to handle the conflict and tension. They may feel they are being unprofessional in risking disruptions in staff relationships. Such relationships are viewed as lying within the domain of the headteacher's traditional authority. Respect for that authority once again appears to clash with a commitment to critical openness. I once noted (see Elliott *et al*. 1979) that: 'Headteachers tend to be anxious about staff expertise at conducting action research in problem areas which are sensitive within their schools.' One headteacher, for example, wanted to be sure the teacher researchers 'had sufficient expertise' to make the results of their research acceptable to the rest of the staff. One way of resolving the dilemma is for teacher researchers to allow the headteacher to have the final say on either the area to be researched or the way research data and findings are used in the school. The temptation to collude with hierarchical decisions about the research focus and use of findings is not confined to reporting inside the school. It also covers reportage beyond the boundaries of the school. Thus we find Ebbutt endorsing the right of his headteacher to determine the conditions under which data collected in the school is shared

> in order to stimulate staff discussion DE requested permission to 'publish' some observations by pinning them on the staffroom notice board. This was rejected, probably quite rightly, by the head on the grounds that the room was also used by evening centre staff.

Ebbutt requested permission from the head to pin data up in the staffroom and accepted the refusal as reasonable, including the assumption that evening centre staff were outsiders rather than insiders. The head's decision not to allow him to pin data up in the staffroom is one thing, but giving him the right to take such a decision by soliciting his permission is quite another thing. Even if the decision was a reasonable one, why should a head be in a better position to make such a decision than the insider researcher? Giving heads and other members of the professional hierarchy an automatic right to determine the conditions under which data is professionally shared pre-empts a full discussion, amongst professional peers, of alternative strategies which could be employed to handle anticipated misuses of data, and the conflicts and tensions they manifest.

The assumption that headteachers ought to control the flow of information between teachers, both within and between schools, is based on an acceptance

of the traditional structure of authority implicit in the craft culture. Territoriality defines spheres of authority. The teacher's sphere is the classroom, while
the head's sphere is the school as a social organization. The transition from a
craft culture to a reflective culture challenges this territorial structure of
authority. Within a reflective practical culture the development of classroom
practice cannot operate effectively under a separate control system from that of
institutional development. They are simply two aspects of a unified process in
which teachers collaboratively develop their practices by deliberating about
both their pedagogical and organizational aspects. Teachers have to relinquish
control over their traditional territory, and headteachers have to relinquish
control over theirs. In this context the headteacher's role is one of orchestrat-
ing a process of collaborative deliberation and decision-making amongst
professional staff.

This vision of schools as participatory democracies is tacitly embedded in the
action-research movement. It may appear to be hopelessly unrealistic in
contexts where the growth of centralized educational systems appears to
unleash a tide of managerialism which turns headteachers into line managers
of the technocratic state. However, I have argued in Chapter 7 that this situation
creates conditions for the emergence of a creative counter-culture. Within a
technocratic system the traditional authority of the headteacher, defined in
terms of his/her experience and expertise as a teacher, is transformed into the
role of managing resources to achieve prescribed outputs. (S)he becomes a
manager rather than a leader of professionals. But the emergence of a reflective
counter-culture offers heads an alternative vision of professional leadership, a
perspective from which to resist simply becoming a functionary of the state.
Teacher researchers who succumb to the temptation of reinforcing traditional
structures of authority in schools diminish the capacity of headteachers to resist
creatively the pressures on them to opt out of their professional leadership role
by reconstructing it.

**4 Teacher researchers in schools tend to opt for quantitative
methods of data collection, such as questionnaires, in preference
to qualitative methods, such as naturalistic observations and
interviews, because the latter involve 'personalized' situations in
which colleagues and pupils find it difficult to divorce an
individual's position and role as researcher from his/her other
positions and roles within the school (see Elliott *et al.* 1979)**

A similar point is made by Simons (1978) when she observes that teachers
prefer to use questionnaires in order 'to distance themselves from the
potentially disturbing effects interviewing and observing can have on personal
relationships in a school.' She argues that teachers do not automatically build
their research role on 'natural practice' by exercising the very same skills and
qualities which make them good teachers. As teacher researchers they tend to

distrust these skills and qualities, preferring to switch into 'what they assume is the role of the researcher, adopting the canons of practice they perceive to be those of the researcher.' In this way the 'teacher' identity is split off from the 'researcher' identity in segregated roles rather than being unified within a single teacher/researcher role by a set of qualities and skills which are generic to it. The problem of building research on 'natural practice' is very well illustrated by James and Ebbutt (1980):

> A particular problem is posed for the teacher-researcher in that he has access to a constant flow of data merely by being present in the school. The same is true of any participant observer, of course, but usually other participants are aware that the observer is doing research. Whilst pupils and colleagues may be aware that a teacher is engaged in research they may divulge things to him as a teacher that they would not want noted by him as a researcher. How is the teacher-researcher to know which role he is perceived to have at any one time, and how is he to handle the resulting data? This is not a problem that we felt we resolved to our total satisfaction.

One way of trying to resolve the problem James and Ebbutt cite is to segregate researcher and teacher and thereby formalize and depersonalize data-gathering methods. I would argue that the problem and this particular solution to it are indicative of a dilemma. The dilemma lies in apparently conflicting values; namely, between the right to privacy and the right to know. As teacher the insider researcher feels under an obligation not to record or report information gathered as a participant in the everyday life of the school. Such information carries the status of private knowledge. The obligation not to report it applies as much to disclosure inside as outside the institution. Reporting consists of either the circulation of a written document or verbal disclosure in a formal setting, such as a meeting, where the information may influence decision-making. The verbal sharing of information in informal settings about each other's practices does not in itself infringe the right to privacy. Shared knowledge of this kind carries the status of 'open secrets'. But, from the standpoint of the craft culture, the thing insiders should not do is to document open secrets or disclose them in formal decision-making settings. It is not information to be used as a basis for calling colleagues to account for their practice. This would amount to an infringement of their professional autonomy and undermine their status as experts.

The norms which constitute the right to privacy are embedded in the professional craft culture of teachers. The only way of reconciling these norms with the gathering and reporting of information in public form is for insiders to take on the persona of the outsider researcher, a stance which allows peers individual control of what they disclose about their activities. This control is enhanced when the data-gathering instruments minimize interpersonal interaction with the insider researchers and enable the identity of individuals providing the data to be hidden. Quantitative methods, which are designed to produce aggregated data in depersonalized and decontextualized form, appear to constitute the perfect solution to the 'insider researchers' dilemma. They generate public knowledge in a form which makes it impossible to use for the purpose of calling individual practitioners to account.

The problem with this way of resolving the dilemma is that decontextualized, impersonal, and aggregated information has only a limited use as a data base which feeds practical judgements and decisions about how to improve educational practices in particular contexts, involving an identifiable group of individual practitioners. Action research involves the collection, analysis and reporting of case data. The more useful the case studies, the more they will need to document practices in context, and this imposes limits on the extent to which personal indentities can be hidden. The individual's right to privacy just doesn't appear to be consistent with the methodological requirements of a collaborative reflective practice grounded in action research. Within a reflective professional culture 'teacher' and 'researcher' are two aspects of a single role in which teaching constitutes a form of research and research constitutes a form of teaching.

Resisting the temptation to embrace quantitative research methods, in order to accommodate a right to privacy within the methodology of insider research, does not imply that teacher researchers have an automatic right to collect, document or report insider information. Procedures and strategies for protecting individuals from possible misrepresentations and misuses of sensitive data, by either the researchers or their 'audiences', certainly need to be developed by insider researchers and discussed with those 'at risk' from their activities, e.g.:

- Cross-checking eyewitness accounts of events and observations.
- Giving individuals opportunities to reply to accounts of their activities and views, and have these incorporated into documents and reports.
- Presenting alternative descriptions, interpretations and explanations of events and practices.
- Consulting individuals about the contexts in which their actions and views are represented and reported.

Procedures like these do not reflect a compromise with a right to privacy. They are consistent with a right to know but, rather than being grounded in the kind of interprofessional mistrust which motivates a switch from teacher into the role of a 'detached and objective' researcher, they are based on considerations which establish conditions for promoting *trust in the researcher as insider* and the value of critical openness within the professional culture. The considerations I refer to are those of *fairness*, *accuracy* and *comprehensiveness*.

5 Teacher researchers, with the exception of those linked to award bearing courses in institutions of higher education, are reluctant to produce case studies of their reflective practices

From my experience of working with teacher researchers in schools, I would argue that the reluctance paradoxically coincides with a strong desire for professional acknowledgement from within and beyond their institutions, of their role as reflective practitioners. Simons (1978) observes that 'Teachers distrust the generalizability of their work.' They assume that case studies are low in generalizability, being therefore of little practical interest to other teachers working in different curriculum areas, schools, sectors, social environments, etc. The dilemma consists in wanting to report something interesting to professional colleagues and peers while believing that there is little of general interest to report.

The assumption that qualitative case studies are low in generalizability is derived from the empiricist tradition which has dominated the academic culture of educational researchers. From the standpoint of this tradition generalizability depends on the extent to which data can be statistically aggregated. However, the assumption just happens to legitimate the values embedded in the traditional craft culture of teachers. It reinforces the values of privacy, territoriality and authority. If insiders research is non-generalizable beyond the specific circumstances it addresses, then it cannot render the expertise of other professionals, operating in other circumstances, problematic. The 'secret garden' is preserved and the influence and spread of insider research contained.

Reflective teachers would do well to engage in a little meta-reflection on how they deliberate about what to do in a particular situation. I have already suggested that they compare and contrast it with cases drawn from their past experience. They develop their understanding of the present case by discovering the ways in which it is similar to and different from other cases in their experience. In this process teachers assume they can generalize from past to present experience. Then why not also assume that other professionals' case studies can provide vicarious experiences which are generalizable to their own situations, and vice versa? Simons (1978) observed that teachers distrusted the generalizability of case studies 'until they read case studies written by peers'. Giving 'reluctant' teachers access to a conversation about other teachers' case studies is a way of helping them to resist the temptation to resolve their reporting dilemma by embracing the empiricist assumption. Like the temptation to embrace the empiricist assumption that objectivity implies quantitative methods (see 4 above), the temptation to embrace an empiricist doctrine about generalizability serves to legitimate ideologically the values embedded in the traditional craft culture.

6 The problem of finding time to undertake research is constantly cited by teacher researchers

Simons (1978) points out that teachers involved in 'insider research/evaluation' activities see themselves first and foremost as classroom teachers: 'Their first loyalty, in primary schools, is to the pupils and in secondary schools to their subjects.'

The problem of time for insider research tends to be viewed as a teaching v. research dilemma which gets resolved in favour of the former. In discussing their personal experience of the problem, James and Ebbutt are sympathetic to such a resolution, in spite of having come to regard 'critical reflection about, and research into, practice as an integral part of the teacher's professional role.' Given the situation that schools as institutions do not prioritize teachers' time in terms of opportunities for reflection on practice, James and Ebbutt argue that 'it is unrealistic to expect all other teachers to be any more altruistic, than we were . . .' In the light of their own school-based research experience they were not surprised 'that many teachers consider school-based research an optional extra, albeit a desirable one, to be engaged in if and when other commitments allow.'

It appears that, for James and Ebbutt, the vision of teaching as a unified reflective practice awaits changes in the organizational prioritizing of teacher time before it can be realized on a large scale. One wonders where the pressure for such organizational change can come from, if not from teachers actively attempting, as part of the action research enterprise itself, to change the organizational structures which prioritize their time. Resolving the problem of time by succumbing to a temptation to split off the research role as an optional extra, simply reinforces organizational structures which support the values and norms of the craft culture. Simons (1978) argues that:

> The citing of time as a constraint on initiating self-evaluation in a school is realistic given the current pattern of organization of curriculum but may also be constructed as a failure to reconsider reallocation of priorities.

James and Ebbutt appear to favour the first interpretation, whereas I prefer the latter. I am very sympathetic to the plight of a small band of insider researchers confronting an alien institutional culture. But surely there are strategies even they can develop to creatively resist organizational constraints on their prioritizing of time. They can, for example, refuse to be co-opted into those organizational maintenance roles which undermine the development of reflective practice, because they reproduce the values and norms of the traditional craft culture. They can refuse to solve methodological problems of insider research by divorcing data-gathering processes from the natural ways of gathering and processing data they use in their work as teachers. Such a stance may help them to reconceive the meaning of 'time for research' and thereby illuminate previously unanticipated opportunities for influencing the ways in which time is organized institutionally. Finally, a small band of isolated teacher researchers can tap into a reflective counter culture in the form of an action-research network which transcends school boundaries and is linked to a teacher-education institution. Membership of such a network can provide the kind of cultural resources which strengthen the capacity of aspiring teacher researchers to resist the time pressures operating on them from inside their schools.

I have tried in this chapter to describe some of the major dilemmas teachers face in attempting to initiate curriculum change in schools through 'insider' action research. In doing so I have pinpointed temptations to resolve these dilemmas in ways which limit and undermine the transformation of the professional culture into one capable of supporting the reflective development of educational practice in schools.

Teacher educators from higher education can do much to support and sustain the growth of a reflective professional culture in schools, which includes fostering the methodological self-reflection so essential for resolving dilemmas of insider research in ways which transform the professional culture rather than reinforce its traditional values and norms.

I have indicated the ways in which teacher researchers have employed some of the methodological assumptions which underpin empiricist methods of academic research to legitimate the traditional values of authority, privacy and territoriality. Even qualitative methodologies developed in academe as alternatives to empiricism can carry over sufficient of its assumptions to render them suspect as models for insider research. For example, Simons (1985) argues that MacDonald's (1974) concept of 'democratic case study' in practice involved: 'treating the case as a cellular structure of privatized information, negotiating access and release of information with each individual guardian.'

I would do well to remember that it was academics like myself and Simons who sold this concept to insider researchers like James and Ebbutt. Methodologies developed on the presumption that the researcher's role is that of an impartial spectator do not easily fit the logic of reflective practice and minimize disruptions to the professional culture caused by research interventions. My dilemma analysis supports the case Simons (1985) now argues: namely, for a distinctive methodology of insider research/evaluation, which rests 'upon the possibility of dismantling the value structure of privacy, territory and hierarchy, and substituting the values of openness, shared critical responsibility and rational autonomy.'

Academic teacher educators have access to intellectual traditions from which they could help insider researchers to construct a distinctive model of inquiry. However, in doing so, they will also need to transform teacher education into a reflective practice, lest they unwittingly transmit assumptions which legitimate traditional professional values and, in doing so, perpetuate the hegemony of the impartial spectators from academe over the production of public knowledge about education.

Simons believes that the transformation in professional values, widened by
the growth of insider research, calls for 'a corresponding degree of insulation'
from the technocratic systems of external surveillance and control currently
evolving within the UK in response to accountability pressures. She cites
MacDonald's (1978) idea of schools as 'self-critical communities within high
walls – groups who risk enough in collective self-reflection to be spared the
added risk of continuous exposure to outside observation.' Exactly what forms
and degrees of insulation from technocratic systems of surveillance and
control teacher researchers will need in order to resist creatively the deprofes-
sionalizing influences of such systems is a matter which all those who are
committed to supporting teacher-initiated change in schools need urgently
to address.

6

A practical guide to action research

A model of the action-research process is outlined, followed by a list of methods and techniques for gathering and analysing data. The final sections of the chapter look at the problem of managing time for action research in schools and the uses to which case reports can be put in fostering school development and accountability.

Action-research might be defined as '*the Study of a social situation with a view to improving the quality of action within it.*' It aims to feed practical judgement in concrete situations, and the validity of the 'theories' or hypotheses it generates depends not so much on 'scientific' tests of truth, as on their usefulness in helping people to act more intelligently and skilfully (see Appendix 2 for examples). In action-research 'theories' are not validated independently and then applied to practice. They are validated through practice.

Lewin's model of action research

The term 'action research' was first coined by the social psychologist Kurt Lewin (see Kemmis 1980). Lewin's model involves a 'spiral of cycles'. Kemmis represents the spiral as shown in Fig. 6.1.

The basic cycle of activities is IDENTIFYING A GENERAL IDEA, RECONNAISSANCE, GENERAL PLANNING, DEVELOPING THE FIRST ACTION STEP, IMPLEMENTING THE FIRST ACTION STEP, EVALUATION, REVISING THE GENERAL PLAN. From this basic cycle the researchers then *spiral* into DEVELOPING THE SECOND ACTION STEP, IMPLEMENTATION, EVALUATION, REVISING GENERAL PLAN, DEVELOPING THE THIRD ACTION STEP, IMPLEMENTATION, EVALUATION and so on.

A revised model

Although I think Lewin's model is an excellent basis for starting to think about what action research involves, it can, as set out above, allow those who use it to assume that 'the general idea' can be fixed in advance, that 'reconnaissance' is merely fact-finding, and that 'implementation' is a fairly straightforward process. But I would argue that:

- The general idea should be allowed to shift.
- Reconnaissance should involve analysis as well as fact-finding and should constantly recur in the spiral of activities, rather than occur only at the beginning.
- Implementation of an action step is not always easy, and one should not proceed to evaluate the effects of an action until one has monitored the extent to which it has been implemented.

In the light of these criticisms I would elaborate the spiral of activities as shown in Fig. 6.2.

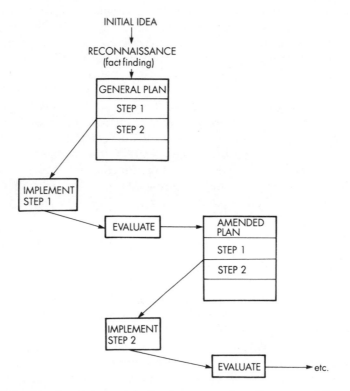

Figure 6.1   Kurt Lewin's model of action research as interpreted by Kemmis (1980).

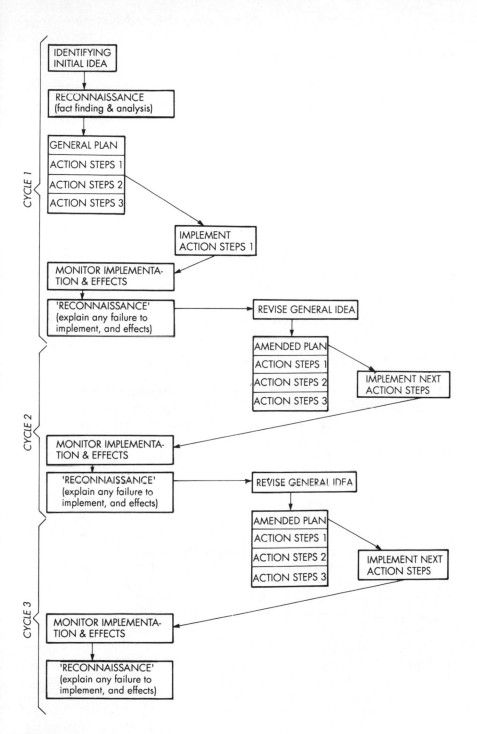

Figure 6.2 A revised version of Lewin's model of action research.

The activities of action research

What follows are descriptions of the activities involved in the action-research cycle. They are similar in many respects to those contained in the Deakin University *Action Research Planner* (see Kemmis *et al.* 1981). However, I have primarily written them in the light of my own experience of trying to help teachers do action-research.

1 Identifying and clarifying the general idea

The 'general idea' is essentially a statement which links an idea to action. Kemmis and others (1981) provide the following examples:

- Students are dissatisfied with the methods by which they are assessed. How can we collaborate to improve student assessment?
- Students seem to waste a lot of time in class. How can I increase the time students spend 'on task'?
- Parents are fairly keen to help the school with the supervision of students' homework. How can we make their help more productive?

In other words the 'general idea' refers to a state of affairs or situation one wishes to change or improve on.

Kemmis and his co-workers warn one to avoid 'issues which you can do nothing about'. They argue that 'Questions like the relationship between socio-economic status and achievement, between ability and a tendency to ask questions in class, may be *interesting* but they have tenuous links with action.' I don't accept this advice entirely. There are certainly ideas which cannot easily be linked with one's actions and should be avoided, even though one may find them theoretically interesting.

However, there are states of affairs which one can link with actions but remain unsure about the extent to which something can be done about them. For example, if pupils are dissatisfied with the way they are assessed this obviously affects a teacher's capacity to help them learn. But he or she may feel that the mode of assessment which prevails is something little can be done about. Nevertheless it is worth the teachers suspending judgement for a time in order to explore whether there is some action he or she could take which would ameliorate the worst effects of the system he or she is constrained to operate with.

The important criteria for selecting a 'general idea' are whether the situation it refers to (a) impinges on one's field of action and (b) is something one would like to change or improve on. The extent to which one is able to change or improve on it is a question which action research should address, rather than assume an answer to.

Another thing to take into account in selecting a general idea as a focus is that one may have misunderstood the nature of the problem, or what needs to be improved. Thus pupils' dissatisfaction with the way they are assessed may merely be a symptom of a much deeper problem, which may 'come to light' during the course of action research. In this case a teacher would want to undertake subsequent actions which tackle that deeper problem rather than merely treat the symptom. The original general idea may need to be constantly revised during the process of action research. This is why I have allowed for this possibility in every cycle of the spiral, rather than 'fixing' the focus for the research at its beginning.

2 Reconnaissance

This activity can be sub-divided into:

(a) Describing the facts of the situation

One needs to describe as fully as possible the nature of the situation one wants changed or improved on. For example, if the problem is 'pupils wasting time in class' one will want to know things like:

- Which pupils are wasting time?
- What are they doing when they are wasting time?
- Are they wasting time doing similar or different things?
- What should they be doing when they are wasting time?
- What are they doing when they are not wasting time?
- Is there a particular point in the lesson, or time of day, or set of topics, where pupils waste time the most?
- What are the different forms in which 'wasting time' manifests itself?

All these facts help to clarify the nature of the problem. The collection of this information can provide a basis for classifying the relevant facts, e.g. generating categories for classifying the different kinds of time-wasting which go on.

It can also lead to some fairly radical changes in one's understanding of the original idea. E.g., one may decide in the light of this exercise that many of the things one thought to be time wasting are not, and that many of the things one thought not to be now appear to be 'time wasting'.

(b) Explaining the facts of the situation

Having collected and described the relevant facts one needs to explain them. How do they arise? What are the relevant contingencies, or critical factors, which have a bearing on the state of affairs described?

In asking these questions one moves from a *description* of the facts to a *critical analysis* of the context in which they arise. This involves:

(i) *'Brainstorming'* – *generating explanatory hypotheses.*
(ii) *Hypothesis testing.*

An hypothesis may cite a relationship between the facts of the problem situation and some other factor(s) operating in its context.

For example, the following hypotheses about the problems of helping pupils to 'reason independently' in classrooms were generated by researchers and teachers involved in the Ford Teaching Project (see Elliott and Adelman 1976).

Positive reinforcers

Hypothesis: Utterances like 'good', 'interesting', 'right', in response to ideas expressed by pupils can prevent the discussion of alternative ideas, since pupils tend to interpret them as attempts to legitimate the development of some ideas rather than others.

Introducing factual information

Hypothesis: When teachers introduce factual information in person, either in written or verbal form, pupils may be prevented from evaluating it, since they will tend to interpret such interventions as attempts to get them to accept its truth.

Each of the above hypothesis has three ingredients. The first is a description of certain contextual factors, e.g. the teacher's use of terms like 'good', 'interesting', 'right'. The second is a description of either an improvement desired – 'the discussion of alternatives ideas' – or a situation which needs to be changed – pupils not evaluating the information available to them. The third aspect is an explanation for the relationship which is cited in the hypothesis.

Having, through brainstorming around a problem, generated some hypotheses, one can then proceed to gather information which is relevant to testing them. For example, evidence can be gathered about the extent to which one uses terms like 'good', 'interesting', 'right'; their effects on pupils' classroom responses; and the ways pupils interpret their use. The gathering of this evidence may also suggest further explanations of the problem situation, which in turn leads to more gathering of information etc.

Even when one has tested hypotheses and found them to apply, they should retain the status of 'hypotheses' rather than 'conclusions', since one can always encounter instances where they do not apply, and which will prompt a search for more comprehensive explanations. The process of analysis is an endless one, but in action research it must be interrupted for the sake of action. And the point of interruption should be when one has sufficient confidence in the hypotheses to allow them to guide action. Explanations do not tell one what to do, but they do suggest possibilities for action. Thus the 'introducing factual information' hypothesis does not tell one not to introduce factual information in person, and instead to give pupils independent access to it, e.g. looking it up in the library or resource centre. But it does provide some guidance. It suggests, for example, that an alternative strategy would be to make one's expectations of how pupils are to use the information one introduces much clearer to them.

3 Constructing the general plan

The general plan of action should contain:

1 A revised statement of the general idea, which by now is likely to have changed, or at least been clarified further.
2 A statement of the factors one is going to change or modify in order to improve the situation, and the actions one will undertake in this direction, e.g. 'I will modify the way I introduce factual information to pupils by clearly explaining what they are to do with it.'

   Although Lewin's model suggests one action step per cycle should be taken, my own experience tells me that it is often necessary to undertake a cluster of steps every cycle.
3 A statement of negotiations one has had, or will have to conduct with others before undertaking the proposed course of action.

   A teacher may need to negotiate some of the actions he or she proposes with colleagues, or a superior, whose capacity to do their job properly could be influenced by the effects of the proposed changes, or perhaps they will 'carry the can for them', or even intervene unconstructively if not consulted. For example, a proposed change of syllabus might need to be negotiated with the relevant head of department, departmental colleagues, the headteacher, or even pupils and their parents.

   As a general principle the initial action steps proposed should lie within areas where the action researchers have the maximum freedom of decision. Later, if it becomes clear that the only solution to the situation lies in 'negotiated action', then the planning should involve the relevant people. However, it is worth noting on the initial general plan what negotiations will have to occur later if certain actions are to be undertaken.
4 A statement of the resources one will need in order to undertake the proposed courses of action, e.g. materials, rooms, equipment, etc.
5 A statement of the ethical framework which will govern access to and release of information.

   One must ask the question: can the information I gather about other people's activities and views be misused by me and those I disseminate it to (and whom could such misuse harm?)? If the answer is 'yes', then one should try to give people a measure of control over one's access to their activities and views, and over the extent to which the information one gathers should be released to others. The key concepts here are *confidentiality*, *negotiation* and *control*. One should pledge to keep the information confidential to the person concerned until one knows whether one wants to release it. One should then pledge to negotiate release with that person, with the proviso that, if disagreement over the 'release question' persists, they have the final say.

It may not be only those immediately involved in the field of action who should have a say in these matters. Others only indirectly involved may nevertheless be harmed by the misuse of information. For example, a headteacher may have to reap some of the consequences of information released about classroom practices in his or her school. One may therefore need to state clearly what his or her rights over the release of information about the school are.

The general plan therefore should include a description of an ethical framework which has been discussed and agreed with the relevant persons.

4 Developing the next action steps

Here one decides exactly which of the courses of action outlined in the general plan one is going to implement next, and how both the process of implementation and its effects are going to be monitored. It is important to remember the following:

(a) One needs to use monitoring techniques which provide evidence of how well the course of action is being implemented.
(b) One needs to use techniques which provide evidence of *unintended* as well as intended effects.
(c) One needs to use a range of techniques which will enable one to look at what is going on from a variety of angles or points of view.

5 Implementing the next action step(s)

It may take some time to succeed at implementing a course of action. It usually implies changes in all the participants' behaviour. For example, a teacher cannot change his or her role (or some aspect of it) without corresponding changes being made in pupils' roles in the classroom. And this may take time if the proposed action(s) involve a fairly radical shift of teaching role. The length of time necessary to secure implementation may depend on the frequency of contact the teacher has with the group of pupils involved. Or it may depend on the extent to which he or she is able to analyse the cause of the implementation problem. In other words, he or she may have to shift away from simply monitoring the extent to which the action is implemented and undertake some reconnaissance into the underlying causes of the difficulties experienced. As a result the general idea of what the problem is, and what needs to be done about it, may have to be modified or changed.

Even if the action step is implemented with relative ease, it may create troublesome side-effects which require a shift into reconnaissance in order to understand how these arise. And this in turn may require some modifications and changes to the general idea and the general plan of action.

As the action researcher shifts from simply monitoring the implementation and effects of an action step into a period of reconnaissance, he or she may need to select a wider range of monitoring techniques from the battery outlined later in this chapter. Multi-techniques will help to secure a more penetrating grasp of the situation. This is an important time for producing analytic memos (see page 83), and also for rethinking the timetable. When the need for an amended plan of action begins to emerge from the reconnaissance undertaken, the writing of a case-study report (see Chapter 7) can help to generate ideas about future possibilities for action at the next cycle.

Techniques and methods for gathering evidence

Here is a list of techniques and methods which can be used to gather evidence in the reconnaissance and monitoring phases of action research.

Diaries

It is useful to keep a diary on a continuous basis. It should contain personal accounts of 'observations, feelings, reactions, interpretations, reflections, hunches, hypotheses, and explanations' (see Kemmis et al. 1981). Accounts should not merely report the 'bald facts' of the situation, but convey a feeling of what it was like to be there participating in it. Anecdotes; near-verbatim accounts of conversations and verbal exchanges; introspective accounts of one's feelings, attitudes, motives, understandings in reacting to things, events, circumstances; these all help one to reconstruct what it was like at the time.

In the Ford Teaching Project (see Elliott and Adelman 1976) we also suggested to teachers, undertaking their own classroom action research, that pupils should keep diaries. As Kemmis and others (1981) argue, this enables a teacher to compare his or her experience of the situation with that of the pupils. However, it is important to remember that keeping a diary is necessarily a personal and private matter, and that the disclosure of its contents should be under the control of its author. There should be no compulsory collecting in of diaries at the end of lessons. One way of ensuring pupil control is for the teacher and pupils to hold periodic 'evaluation sessions' after each party has read back through the diaries. During the evaluation session each party draws on 'diary evidence' to support the views expressed. But its 'disclosure' remains under the control of the authors. However, there is no reason why diaries could not be 'exchanged' if both parties agree.

Finally, the contents of diaries should be properly dated. In the context of classroom action research, details like form, time, subject, should be cited at the beginning of an entry. Entries may vary in length and amount of detail. They should probably be fullest at those points where the heaviest monitoring and reconnaissance is planned.

Profiles

A profile provides a view of a situation or person over time. In a teaching situation one can produce profiles of lessons, or of the performance of certain pupils. Walker and Adelman's *Guide to Classroom Observation* (1975) gives some excellent examples of lesson profiles. One basic format they suggest can be seen in Table 6.1.

Document analysis

Documents can provide information which is relevant to the issues and problems under investigation. For example, in the context of classroom action research, relevant documents could include:

● Syllabuses and schemes of work.
● 'Curriculum' reports of school working parties and committees.
● Examination papers and tests used.
● Minutes of departmental meetings.
● Work cards and assignment sheets.
● Sections used from textbooks.
● Samples of children's written work.

Photographic evidence

Photographs can capture the visual aspects of a situation. For example, in the context of classroom action research they can visually capture:

Table 6.1   An example of a lesson profile (Walker and Adelman 1975) which can be inserted into diary entries at relevant points

Time

	10 minutes	*20 minutes*	*30 minutes*	*10 minutes*
Teacher Activity	Settling in; giving out books	Introduces experiment; gives directions; asks questions	Moves round helping small groups working on experiments	Clearing up
Pupil activity	Finishing work from last lesson	Listening to teacher's directions; answering questions	Working on experiments	Write up results of experiments
Resources	Text books; pens; exercise books		Bunsen burners; tongs; foodstuffs; balances	Exercise books; pens

- Pupils working on classroom tasks.
- What is going on 'behind the teacher's back'.
- The physical lay-out of the classroom.
- The pattern of social organization in the classroom, e.g. whether pupils are working in groups, or spatially isolated, or sitting in rows facing the teacher.
- The teacher's physical posture and position when talking to children, e.g. sitting down at their level, standing above them.

Some of this evidence can only be secured with the help of an observer, but there is quite a lot the teacher can collect by him or herself.

Photographic evidence can provide a basis for discussion with other members of an action research team or with other participants in the situation under investigation.

Tape/video recordings and transcripts

In the context of classroom action research tape or video can be used to record lessons in whole or in part. Unless video is used by an observer, its use has limitations. Used by the teacher (or pupils), it can be very distracting, although this may diminish as the user becomes more skilful. If the cameras are fixed, they may not be able to pick up certain things which are relevant and important, e.g. the verbal exchanges between the teacher and a particular pupil during a non class-teaching episode.

Portable tape-recorders with built-in microphones are probably less distracting for the teacher to carry around the classroom.

A teacher will probably get more out of a recording if he or she listens to (or looks at) it, *and then* transcribes interesting and relevant episodes. This enables him or her to move backwards and forwards through an episode more quickly and easily than constantly playing the recorder backwards and forwards. However, transcribing by hand is immensely time consuming. Teachers I have worked with testify to the fact that it is well worth the effort. It concentrates the mind on what is happening to a greater degree than simply listening and watching. But restrictions on available time will limit the extent to which transcription is possible.

Using an outside observer

This technique can be useful if the outsider is well briefed by the insider, so that he or she knows the sort of information which will be of use to the latter. In the context of classroom action research the outsider can collect information and convey it to the teacher in the following ways:

- Taking photographs and then passing them over (perhaps with comments attached).
- Making a video-recording and showing the teacher excerpts he or she feels to be significant.

- Making detailed notes as he or she observes, and using them as the basis of a short report for the teacher to read.
- Allowing the teacher to interview him or her; the former using a tape-recorder or taking notes.

The outsider may be a fellow member of the action-research team but operating outside one's immediate field of action; a colleague who is not involved in the research; or an external person who visits the school (or site) as a consultant.

Interviewing

Interviewing is a good way of finding out what the situation looks like from other points of view. I have already mentioned interviewing an observer. But it is also important to interview those one normally interacts with in the situation. In the context of classroom action research a sample of pupils should be interviewed frequently. Eliciting 'authentic' accounts from them is not easy initially, given a teacher's authority position. One way to overcome this is to ask an external consultant to do some initial interviews. He or she, *with the pupils' permission*, can hand over a recorded interview to the teacher who listens to it and subsequently discusses the issues it raises with the pupils. If, in this discussion, the teacher demonstrates a capacity for open-mindedness and impartiality, pupils will be increasingly willing to talk openly with him or her directly. The external intermediary can eventually be dispensed with. An alternative to using an external consultant is to train pupils to interview each other, and for the pupil interviewer to get his peers' permission to hand recordings over to the teacher.

Interviews can be *structured, semi-structured, unstructured*. In the structured interview the questions are preset by the interviewer. In the unstructured interview the initiative for raising the relevant topics and issues is left to the interviewee. Once the latter has raised a topic or issue, the interviewer can then ask him or her to expand, explain or clarify points. A useful device for helping the interviewee to raise issues and topics is for the interviewer to play a recording of the situation which the former then stops at points where he or she would like to talk about something. A similar device would be to use some other kind of evidence as a basis for helping an interviewee to raise topics and issues, e.g. a collection of photographs, a document, etc.

During the initial stages of action research, when one wishes to remain as open as possible on the question of what information is relevant, an unstructured interview format is probably best. Later, when one is clearer about the sort of information which will be relevant, one can shift towards a more structured approach. But even here the interviewer should leave room for the interviewees to raise their own topics and issues. A semi-structured approach, where the interviewer asks certain preset questions but allows interviewees freedom to digress and raise their own topics as the interview progresses (not 'tacked on' at the end), is probably better than a rigidly structured approach.

The running commentary

There are periods in most practical situations where a participant can pause to observe what is going on. This provides an opportunity for producing a running commentary on events. In teaching situations one useful application of this technique is when observing a pupil or group of pupils working at a task.

Observation should continue for at least five minutes. Do not intervene in the task the pupil is (or pupils are) engaged on. Sit as near as possible but try to angle your line of vision at a different angle to that of the pupil(s), e.g. avoid sitting face to face. Avoid any posture or position which highlights the fact that a pupil is (or pupils are) being watched. Try to write down as literally and concretely as possible everything that is said and done. Note things like tone, gesture, etc. Keep the commentary as descriptive as possible, avoiding judgements and high-level interpretations from which it is difficult to tell what was actually happening (e.g. 'they worked well').

The shadow study

Here a participant is 'shadowed' for a period of time, and a continuous running commentary made on his or her actions and reactions.

In classroom situations the person shadowed could be a teacher or a pupil (as he or she moves through a series of lessons). The observer doing the shadowing may be an external consultant or on-site colleague. The observations could even be shared between members of the action-research team. Each member would take turns to shadow the subject at different points. Later the team could meet to put their observations together.

Observers should be briefed on the kinds of things to look for, and their reports made available to the action researchers (if the latter have commissioned outsiders to do them).

Checklists, questionnaires, inventories

Checklists are basically sets of questions one answers onself. They structure observations by indicating the kinds of information needed to answer the questions. An exclusive reliance on checklists can blinker one to unanticipated effects of actions, and factors in their context which may explain these effects.

Checklists should always be used in conjunction with more open and less structured techniques of monitoring, e.g. recordings, free observation, running commentaries, unstructured interviews.

This recommendation also applies to questionnaires and inventories. Both are ways of eliciting other people's observations and interpretations of situations and events, as well as their attitudes towards them. But again others may have important observations, interpretations, etc., to make which one hasn't anticipated in designing these instruments.

A questionnaire is basically a list of questions one wants to ask other people. It is one way of checking whether other participants in the situation would give the same answers to the kind of questions one has asked oneself on a checklist.

An inventory is a list of statements about a situation which others may agree with or not. Responses can consist of a tick placed in one of the following categories: Strongly agree – agree – uncertain – disagree – strongly disagree. An inventory is quite a good way of discovering the extent to which others agree or disagree with one's observations and interpretations.

Questionnaires and inventories allow one to quantify people's observations, interpretations and attitudes. They should be used as follow-up techniques to more qualitative ones. For example, I once interviewed a small sample of parents at a school on what they valued about schools. In these unstructured interviews I discovered to my surprise that more than half the parents placed such considerations as 'concerned about children's personal and social as well as their academic development', 'children are happy there', 'teachers care about individuals', way above my anticipated responses, namely, 'good exam results', 'good discipline' and 'uniform'. If I had started with a questionnaire or inventory I would probably have missed out some of the former considerations. But, having elicited these considerations through unstructured interviews, I then incorporated them into an inventory which was circulated to a larger, more representative, sample. This enabled me to assess how widely the particular values cited in interviews were shared by other parents of the school in question.

In my view inventories, scaled in the way indicated, are better than questionnaires as techniques for gathering data which complements that collected through unstructured or semi-structured interviews. As Winter (1982) has pointed out, the latter enable people to express ambivalent views, and so can inventories to some extent. But questionnaires tend to force people to present their views as if they were quite unambivalently held.

Triangulation

Triangulation (see Elliott and Partington 1975, for an example) is not so much a technique for monitoring, as a more general method for bringing different kinds of evidence into some relationship with each other so that they can be compared and contrasted.

The basic principle underlying the idea of triangulation is that of collecting observations/accounts of a situation (or some aspects of it) from a variety of angles or perspectives, and then comparing and contrasting them. For example, as a teacher one can compare and contrast accounts of teaching acts in the classroom from one's own, the pupils' and an observer's point of view.

The accounts may be elicited through interviews, the submission of written reports, photographs, etc.

In comparing different accounts, the points where they *differ*, *agree* and *disagree* should be noted. In cases of disagreement one can check against evidence contained in recordings and transcripts. It is also desirable to mount discussions on points of disagreement between the various parties involved; preferably under the chairmanship of a 'neutral' party.

Triangulation of evidence is an excellent preliminary to the production of an analytic memo.

Analytic memos

Analytic memos contain one's systematic thinking about the evidence one has collected and should be produced periodically, normally at the end of a period of monitoring or reconnaissance. These memos may record such things as:

- New ways of conceptualizing the situation under investigation which have emerged.
- Hypotheses which have emerged and which one would perhaps like to test further.
- Citations of the kind of evidence you need to collect in the future, in order to 'ground' emergent concepts and hypotheses more fully.
- Statements about emerging problems and issues within one's field of action.

The analyses contained in these memos, which may be as short as one or two pages, should be cross-referenced to the relevant evidence on which they are based, e.g. to certain entries in the diary, or to sections of transcribed tape/video recordings.

Finding time for gathering evidence

In selecting techniques for gathering evidence one needs to consider how much time one can realistically set aside for it. Here it is useful to think in terms of what Len Almond at Loughborough University calls 'containable time' (see James 1982).

For example, with respect to classroom action research a teacher should decide exactly when, and how much, time can be set aside for monitoring his next action step(s) and its effects. It is no good collecting more evidence than one can afford to process and reflect about. And it is no good deciding to transcribe all recordings when one knows one hasn't the time to do it. So how many lessons are monitored and which techniques are selected should all be matched to a realistic estimate of available time. The 'matching' process is helped by the working out of a timetable. Kemmis *et al.* (1981) suggest the format in Table 6.2.

Table 6.2 Timetable format suggested by Kemmis *et al.* (1981)

Stage	Beginning/ closing date	Monitoring	Duration	Comments
Finalizing General Plan	24.4.81–1.5.81			Availability of tape-recorder to be finalized. X to agree to swap rooms
First action step	4.5.81–15.5.81	*Tape record* 20 minutes of Year 1CB Science in the two single periods each week. *Write impressions* in spare period which follows (diary) Interview students (three to begin with) for impressions	Two weeks, four · lessons	Allow two periods on Friday 1 p.m. to edit tape. (Just write out questions and answers.) Collate with impressions (mine and students).
Evaluation	After vacation		One week	Verbal report to science faculty first Friday after vacation: 5.6.81

Organizing and reporting action research in schools

In describing the action-research cycle I have largely illustrated the activities involved and the research techniques available with examples from classroom action research. But the activities and techniques described apply to any research undertaken by people with a view to improving their own actions in social situations. Even in the context of educational institutions action research has applications beyond the study of classrooms. For example, it can be used to improve the management of schools, the pastoral care system, teacher–parent communication, etc., etc. However, since my interest in writing this chapter is mainly to provide a framework for school-based classroom research, I shall confine the remarks which follow to this context. They will consist of a series of answers to questions I believe to be important when organizing action research in schools.

How long should one take to complete 'a cycle'?

One can give no firm answer to this. There is a danger of forcing the process through when the situation requires one to sustain an activity for perhaps a longer period than originally anticipated. For example, implementation efforts are often abandoned on the basis of a very superficial analysis of the problems. The analysis is confined to the quite inadequate amount of time estimated for implementing the course of action.

However, one has to anticipate roughly how long an activity or cycle will take to complete satisfactorily. One can then readjust one's original timetable in the light of experience.

In the UK the fact that school terms are usually interspersed by fairly long vacations suggests that this is at least a natural organizational unit of time in which to complete a 'cycle' of classroom action-research activity. Given a fourteen-week term, 'a cycle' might be timetabled as in Table 6.3.

How long should one continue the spiral before terminating heavy monitoring, and perhaps shifting the focus of the research on to another problem area?

Again one cannot legislate for this, but I would normally feel it necessary to complete at least three, and perhaps four, cycles before one ought to be sufficiently satisfied with the improvements effected. In the context of classroom action research this could well mean a commitment of at least a year.

One may, however, discover after one or two cycles that further improvements cannot be made without the co-operation and intervention of others outside the research team. For example, in a classroom context, one may decide that something needs to be done about the organizational context of classroom practice. Perhaps changes need to be made which are beyond one's powers to make, e.g. the syllabus, or in timetabling arrangements, or in the ways pupils are grouped. In such cases the research team in the school should move into a period of negotiation with the relevant persons, committees, etc., who control what needs changing. Usually these changes cannot be made overnight and negotiations need to proceed sufficiently in advance, in school normally during the Easter Term.

While these external negotiations are going on, the spiral of action research should focus on them directly, and away from classroom action. But one should use the evidence collected on classroom action as the basis for the negotiations which are now to be monitored.

Should the general plan and decisions about monitoring be an individual or team effort?

This will depend on whether the group engaged in the research is working in the *same* or a *similar* situation. For example, if the group is 'team teaching' the

Table 6.3 Sample timetable for an action-research cycle

	Wk	Activity	Monitoring	Duration	Comments
Cycle 1	1	Clarifying general idea			Team meeting
	2 3 4	Reconnaissance	Class 4T: keep diary for all lessons. Tape-record in one lesson per week, and collect samples of written work and assignment cards for these lessons	One lesson per week (with exception of keeping diary)	
	5 6	General plan	Diary (4T)		Write an analytic memo and begin to formulate plan
	7	HALF TERM BREAK			Write first draft of general plan
	8	General plan	Diary (4T)		Discuss general plan at team meeting
	9 10	Develop action steps 1	Diary (4T)		Write timetable for monitoring in weeks 11–14
	11 12 13 14	Implementing action steps 1	Diary (4T) (+ techniques selected at weeks 9–10)	Two lessons per week / One lesson per week	Study evidence collected. Write analytic memo to share at team meeting.

Wk	Activity	Monitoring	Duration	Comments
15				
16	VACATION:	Write case study (3,000 words maximum + case record) for team meeting in week 1 next term		
17				
Cycle 2 18				
19				
20				
21				
22				
23				
24				
25				

same pupils, then decisions should be a group responsibility. But, if the group consists of teachers working with different classes (although they share a common problem), then the decisions should be individual ones. However, there will be courses of action individuals can undertake together, and it is important therefore, that they keep roughly in step with each other. This will also enable a profitable sharing of insights and research strategies to take place. A group working in different, but similar, classroom situations should have a co-ordinator who:

(a) Convenes approximately three team meetings per cycle, e.g. at the beginning, middle and end of a term.
(b) Keeps a record of any agreed general plan which emerges.
(c) Co-ordinates negotiations between individual team-members and the headteacher, other staff, external consultants, etc.
(d) Helps individuals to share insights and research strategies.
(e) Co-ordinates the writing up of research reports and papers.

The initial meeting in a cycle should be to clarify the problem situation, perhaps by discussing case studies on the previous cycle of activities. What reconnaissance needs to be done in order to understand the situation in greater depth should also be discussed. The middle meeting should discuss (or finalize) the general plan(s), and the end-of-cycle meeting should study analytic memos on 'implementation problems and effects'.

Reporting action research

Case studies are a way of publicly reporting action research to date. Ideally case-study reports should be based on analytic memos. At least one full report should be written at the point where one decides to end a particular spiral of action and research and switch to a quite different issue or problem.

A case-study report of action research should adopt a historical format; telling the story as it has unfolded over time. It should include (but not necessarily in separate sections) accounts of:

- How one's 'general idea' evolved over time.
- How one's understanding of the problem situation evolved over time.
- What action steps were undertaken in the light of one's changing understanding of the situation.
- The extent to which proposed actions were implemented, and how one coped with the implementation problems.
- The intended and unintended effects of one's actions, and explanations for why they occurred.
- The techniques one selected to gather information about (a) the problem situation and its causes, and (b) the actions one undertook and their effects.
- The problems one encountered in using certain techniques and how one resolved them.
- Any ethical problems which arose in negotiating access to, and release of, information, and how one tried to resolve them.
- Any problems which arose in negotiating action steps with others, or in negotiating the time, resources and co-operation one wanted during the course of the action research.

This checklist is a revised version of one proposed by Kemmis *et al.* (1981).

Stenhouse (1978) has made a useful distinction between *case study*, *case record* and *case data*. In the context of action research the case data will consist of all the evidence one collects, e.g. in the form of recordings, transcripts, diaries, notes, photographs, etc. The case record will consist of an ordered selection of evidence from the case data, which is organized in terms of its relevance to the issues addressed in the case study. The case study is essentially an analysis of one's experience to date. At points one should cross-reference the analysis to the evidence on which it is based; the 'primary sources'.

After the case study is written, this evidence can be ordered into the case record. The existence of the latter enables the reader to check the interpretations and explanations contained in the case study against their primary sources.

Making use of case studies and case records

Action research enables schools to reconcile self-evaluation for accountability purposes with self-evaluation for professional development. The case studies and case records generated through action research can provide the basis on which accounts of educational practice are constructed for discussion with others. The others may be internal or external to the school. Here are a few fictional examples of ways in which case studies and case records can be used.

Example 1: Internal

A teacher used his case study as a basis for discussing his classroom practice with colleagues at a departmental meeting.

Example 2: Internal

A co-ordinator of an action-research team was asked by the senior management of a school to report on an issue it was concerned about and believed to be well documented in the team's case studies. The co-ordinator subsequently examined the case studies and records in the light of this issue and produced a report which was then discussed with the senior management.

Example 3: External

The governing body requested a report on 'classroom issues' from the school for its next meeting. The headteacher asked the classroom action-research team in the school to produce it. They compared and contrasted each other's case studies and case records and extracted 'general issues'. Then each member of the team produced a short 'general account' of an issue, and the resulting accounts were put together by the co-ordinator for presentation to the governing body.

Example 4: External

A parent–teacher association (PTA) had expressed reservations about the teaching of basics in the school. The result was the initiation of an action-research project on the subject. The team involved produced a 'general issues' report after comparing and contrasting their case studies. The report was discussed at the annual general meeting of the PTA.

Such uses of case studies and case records could foster a greater integration of accountability and professional development activities. Not only would the products of action research contribute to accountability, but the discussion stimulated by their use would also feed back into the reflection taking place 'where the action is'.

Part III
Action research in policy contexts

7

Action research and the emergence of teacher appraisal in the UK

This chapter looks at some of the ambiguities surrounding negotiations over another government initiative: teacher appraisal. It analyses a well-known 'practical guide' and shows how the process it describes technologizes teaching and hierarchically controls teachers' conceptions of their practice. In contrast the author outlines an alternative two-tier model of appraisal grounded in an action-research process and argues that actual examples of its emergence as a response to the threat of hierarchical control can be found in schools. The emergence of action research as the basis for an alternative approach to teacher appraisal is explained in terms of the theory of 'creative resistance' (referred to earlier in Chapter 4 but considered in greater depth in this chapter).

In England and Wales teachers in schools and universities are increasingly coming to accept performance appraisal as a fact of life. The government has finally decided to implement it as a matter of national policy for schools. The government's conciliation service (ACAS) constituted the national mechanism by which agreed frameworks were originally negotiated between employers (vice-chancellors and principals in the case of university teachers and local education authorities in the case of school teachers) and teachers' professional associations.

I have described elsewhere (Elliott 1987) the transformation in the political rhetoric of teacher appraisal in schools during the period between the publication of the government's White Paper on 'Teaching Quality' (DES 1983) and the ACAS-negotiated agreement (DES/ACAS 1987). The White Paper quite unambiguously proposed appraisal as a strategy of hierarchical surveillance and control over the work of teachers, fulfilling such management functions as discovering grounds for dismissal, providing a rationale for redeployment and merit pay, and identifying training needs.

The response from teachers was a hostile one. Much of the resulting controversy centred around the 'legitimate purposes' of appraisal rather than the idea in itself. Teachers and their organizations emphasized classroom-focused professional learning, together with career development, as the primary purposes of appraisal. They also argued for the right of appraisees to exercise a high measure of control over access to and use of appraisal records. All of these ideas were eventually incorporated, in some shape or form, into the ACAS-negotiated agreement. The later controversy over appraisal in universities proceeded along similar lines, culminating in not dissimilar trade-offs between what one might crudely dichotomize as the cultures of 'managerialism' and 'professionalism'.

The possibility of creative conformity

The study of negotiations, over both the appraisal of school and university teachers, indicates that teachers are not entirely powerless to resist attempts to transfer control over their professional work and careers into the hands of the managers and administrators of resources. To the extent that policy-makers feel they need to legitimate their policies to those affected by them, they have to accommodate at the level of rhetoric the professional culture of the target group. Of course, a measure of control over the rhetoric of appraisal is not the same as realizing the ideas and values it signifies in practice. But it does give the targets of policy a measure of leverage over how it shapes up in practice.

In the earlier account of appraisal issues referred to above, I asserted that I was 'optimistic enough about human nature to believe that if formal appraisal is part of a broad strategy for transforming schools into systems of coercive power it can be successfully resisted.' Such optimism was based on the belief that teachers do not have infinitely plastic natures. However, I rejected the view that resistance must always manifest itself in forms of rebellion and obstructionism and advocated a stance of 'creative conformity'. It is the rhetoric constructed in attempts to legitimate social policy through negotiated frameworks which make such a stance possible. The 'conformity' stems from adherence in practice to the policy enshrined in the rhetoric. The 'creative' aspect lies in the novel interpretations of policy which can be legitimated by the rhetoric.

Appraisal policies as 'negotiated ambiguities'

From the evidence of the English 'agreements' it would be a mistake to see appraisal policies as clear, coherent and unambiguous guides to practice. Let us first consider a few examples from the ACAS agreement with school teachers. This agreement provided the basis for a national pilot scheme from which an agreed set of procedures were generated by a National Steering Group. These were then broadly endorsed by the Secretary of State.

The nature and purpose of appraisal

The Working Group understands appraisal not as a series of perfunctory periodic events, but as a continuous and systematic process intended to help individual teachers with their professional development and career planning, and to help ensure that the inservice training and deployment of teachers matches the complementary needs of individual teachers and the schools.

The reference to professional development and career planning accommodates a professionally acceptable view of the purpose of appraisal, whereas the reference to deployment and in-service training may accommodate a more managerial perspective. I use the term 'managerial' to signify a particular style of management, namely: one which dispossesses the workforce of the power to control their occupational performance and futures. If appraisal is to foster professional development, then it must enhance personal competence. No professional could object to this, since it suggests increased self-mastery and control over performance. Similarly the purpose of helping professionals with career planning suggest giving them more control over their 'futures'. Inasmuch as facilitating the development of professional competence and careers are legitimate functions of management, the use of appraisal as a tool which enables it to exercise these functions effectively is professionally acceptable. Rather than exercising power over the practices and careers of individuals, this kind of appraisal can professionally empower them.

'Deployment' and 'in-service training' can be interpreted as fostering professional and career development. But they can also be interpreted as destructive forces. 'Deployment' can signify the continuous disruption of careers, and the removal of the individual's powers of self-determination. In this context in-service training shifts its meaning. It becomes a means of reskilling individuals to occupy the job slots to which they are deployed by managers, rather than a continuing process of developing individuals' capacities to do the things they want to do better.

Who appraises whom? A teacher's immediate supervisor who may be the Headteacher, or other experienced teacher designated by the Headteacher

This principle is also high in ambiguity. It endorses both professional peer appraisal and hierarchical appraisal. It does the former by highlighting the importance of professional experience and thereby rules out non-teachers or beginning teachers. (Indeed, it also rules out student and parent appraisal.) However, the peer appraisal is hierarchized, although the appointment of an 'experienced teacher designated by the Headteacher' offers the option of minimizing the hierarchical relation between appraiser and appraisee. A truly peer appraisal would surely be one in which the selection of appraisers was controlled by the staff group as a whole and not hierarchically.

'. . . the appraisal process needs to be of a continuous nature. Appraisal must not become a bureaucratic chore or a casual paper exercise. Against that background we think that the frequency of formal appraisals culminating in written reports should vary according to the stage of the teacher's career

Again the principle is somewhat ambiguous. Having defined appraisal as an ongoing and non-bureaucratic professional development process, an element of periodic formal appraisal, culminating in the production of written records, is then inserted.

The elements in the appraisal process are self-appraisal, review discussion with appraiser, observation by appraiser, the appraisal interview, appeals against appraisers' judgements, reporting to headteacher

Although there is a tendency to place these elements in a mechanical sequence, the agreement accepts that 'after the introductory phase, many of the items may be run together.' In other words, self-appraisal may be integrated into other elements such as a review of progress, observation and the appraisal interview. Rather than proceed according to an ordered mechanical sequence, some of the items may operate as continuously interacting dimensions of a dynamic process.

What the ambiguous criteria described above do is to permit a degree of latitude over how the appraisal process is to be interpreted in practice, while at the same time accommodating both a professional and a managerial view of its functions. The options with respect to interpretation appear to be about the emphasis placed on one perspective rather than the other.

In commenting on the ACAS document the National Union of Teachers (one of its signatories) argued that it 'was capable of varying interpretation' and therefore the use of the word 'agreement' was not strictly accurate. Indeed the union stated reservations about wording which could be interpreted ambiguously and claimed they were shared by all the teachers' organizations represented on the ACAS Working Party. The reservations were as follows:

1 The reference to the 'deployment of teachers' was capable of 'misinterpretation and subsequent misuse'. The union argued that, whereas in one sense deployment constitutes an aspect of 'successful and acceptable career

development . . . it will bring to mind the process of redeployment to take account of falling rolls . . .'

2 Although the 'agreement' asserts that appraisal would be quite separate from disciplinary procedures, a connection between the two was implicit in the statement that the latter 'might need to draw on relevant information from the appraisal records'.

3 Although the document argues that appraisal reports should be 'regarded as transient, not as a final reckoning', the fact that they are available 'to officers authorized by the CEO (Chief Education Officer)' implies the possibility of unspecified but wide access to them.

The union argued that records should be confidential to appraiser and appraisee, have an agreed life and have access to them controlled by the appraisee. For the purposes of school-based management decisions 'an *appropriate separate extract*' should be made available to the headteacher.

4 The reference concerning the application of appraisal results to the 'LEA management of the teaching force' is ambiguous. If this refers to better-informed arrangements for in-service training, it is highly acceptable. However, teachers might be suspicious that it refers to other things, e.g. forcible redeployment, dismissal, etc.

What is clear is that the unions wished to eliminate ambiguities of expression which allowed managers to use appraisal as an instrument for compulsory redeployment and/or dismissal. The comments embrace a view of the legitimate functions of management in relation to teachers: those of enhancing and supporting their professional and career development. If the unions had succeeded in eliminating these ambiguities altogether from the document, then they would indeed have completely reversed the conception of appraisal expressed in the government's 1983 White Paper. As it stands the ACAS document's ambiguities allowed for the possibility of establishing, at least in the context of the pilot experiments subsequently established in a few LEAs, a model of teacher appraisal in which managerialism is minimized and the management functions of appraisal subordinated to the purposes of professional and career development. Such subordination is most clearly expressed in procedural form by the NUT's view that documentation available to the headteacher for the purpose of school-based management decisions should consist only of extracts from the full appraisal record. This appears to imply a two-tier model, consisting of a first tier of self and peer appraisal and a second-tier management appraisal. The management appraisal is dependent on data gathered in the first-tier process and selected by those involved in it.

I have argued that the 'professional' and 'management' functions of appraisal can only be reconciled through the development in practice of a two-tier model. This view was developed in a paper (see Elliott 1988a) which looked at the implications of the ACAS agreement about staff appraisal in universities. Although the university teachers' document is not entirely lacking in ambiguity

of expression, it does appear to be more explicit about subordinating management functions to teachers' professional and career development. For
example, the stated purposes of appraisal are to:

(a) Help . . . staff to develop their careers within the institution.
(b) Improve staff performance.
(c) Identify changes in the organization or operation of the institution which
      would enable individuals to improve their performance.
(d) Identify and develop potential for promotion.
(e) Improve the efficiency with which the institution is managed.

There is no reference to the ambiguous term 'deployment'. Purpose (d) refers
instead to identifying and developing potential for promotion. Inasmuch as
'deployment' is implicit in this objective, it is expressed in a manner acceptable
to professionals.

   Purpose (c) acknowledges the ways in which organizational contexts can
enable or constrain the development of individuals' practices. Thus appraisal
should involve the appraisee in assessing context as well as performance and
thereby identify for managers changes to organizational/institutional arrangements which will enable staff to improve their practices. Here the management
function of organizational development is clearly subordinated to the aim of
improving professional practices.

   Purpose (e) is perhaps the most obviously ambiguous statement. In one
sense it can simply be interpreted as subordinate to purposes (a) to (d). In
another sense it can legitimate linking appraisal to compulsory redeployment,
dismissal proceedings, etc.

   The criteria outlined in the universities' document also suggest a primary
emphasis on professional and career development. For example, the appraisal
process should:

   (d)   encourage staff to reflect on their own performance, and to take
   steps to improve it;
   (e)   involve an appropriate mixture of self-assessment, informal interviewing and counselling. The appraisal process should be regarded as a
   joint professional task shared between appraiser and appraisee, with the
   latter involved at all stages. The views of students and others who are
   affected by the performance of staff should also be taken into account;
   (f)   provide for an agreed record of discussion, and of follow-up action;
   (g)   provide for staff to record dissent on an otherwise jointly agreed
   appraisal record;
   (h)   provide for a second opinion in any serious case of disagreement
   between appraiser and appraisee;
   (i)   provide for effective follow-up action in relation to staff development needs, weaknesses in organization, provision of resources . . .

In many respects these criteria are similar to those listed in the school-teachers' documents. But the university teachers are even more explicit in emphasizing appraisal as a reciprocal or two-way process characterized by self-reflection, dialogue, and mutual trust. They are at pains to specify procedures to overcome any 'hierarchy of credibility' between the views of appraisers and appraisees. The introduction of a 'second opinion' and 'student feedback' can all be seen as a means to this end. Such possibilities are not specified in the schoolteachers' document.

When it comes to 'Institutional Arrangements' the university teachers' document gives appraisees 'the right to request that an alternative appraiser be appointed' and to agree about the appointment. The document also, like the schools' document, leaves room for non-management personnel to be designated as appraisers. However, in spite of its measures for securing reciprocity in the appraisal process, the relation between appraiser and appraisee is, as in the schoolteachers' document, largely conceived as a hierarchical relation. Even when a manager is not the appraiser, management largely controls selections through a power of designation. This opens the appraisal process to the risk of merely reproducing a hierarchical control over what are to count as credible judgements.

In comparing the school and university 'agreements' I would conclude that the former is rather higher in ambiguity about purposes and procedures. The latter tends to build in more explicit safeguards to counter managerial excess. However, both appear to give considerable leverage to those who wish to develop forms of appraisal which empower teachers to exercise greater control over their performance and careers, and thereby minimise managerial uses of appraisal. Nevertheless, I do not underestimate the fact that ambiguities in both documents are sufficient to give a considerable amount of leverage to those who wish to use appraisal as a system for legitimating managerial control over teachers' work and futures. The leverage lies essentially in the hierarchical relation between appraiser and appraisee, and the way this enables a consensus in judgements to be ideologically rather than rationally constructed, i.e. in a form which legitimates and masks relations of domination between managers and the teaching force.

The ideological construction of appraisals: an example of how it can be done

In this section I will attempt to demonstrate how an appraisal scheme, which appears to satisfy all the criteria specified in the ACAS framework for school teachers, can operate as a ritualistic mechanism for ideological construction. In doing so I shall focus on the practical guide produced by Suffolk County Council Education Department (1987), a local education authority which participated in the national pilot scheme. The guide outlines a concrete process which appears to have the exclusive aim of improving performance at all levels of the hierarchy in schools. There is no mention of using appraisal records for redeploying, dismissing or even making decisions about who should or should not be promoted. Appraisal is also seen as a continuous, cyclical process of staff development in which the formal interview with an appraiser has been redefined as 'the appraisal dialogue' and constitutes only one of its elements.

At each level of the school hierarchy individuals are appraised by their immediate superior, described in the guide as 'their "line manager"'. But hierarchical control over the appraisal process is further reinforced by giving the appraiser's appraiser responsibility for monitoring the appraisee's progress six months after the formal appraisal dialogue. The role of the appraiser's appraiser is known as the appraisee's 'grandparent'. The point of such second-order monitoring by the 'grandparent' is stated as 'a way of ensuring that help and support towards the attainment of targets has been/will be forthcoming'.

Targets are referred to at some point in 11 of the 20 pages in the guide. It is a term which appears to structure each of the five 'practical steps for appraisal' outlined.

At the stage of preparing for the 'appraisal dialogue', the appraiser will consider the appraisee's job, performance, work-related relationships, training/qualifications, past job experiences, attitude and personal matters. A consideration of the job includes 'targets set after last appraisal discussion', and any explicit standards that have been established for assessing the attainment of job-related targets. Considering the appraisee's actual performance includes 'Targets attained or not; ... Reasons for causes of non-attainment; ...' The appraisee's preparation is called 'self-appraisal' and it appears to involve the same range of considerations.

One aspect of the preparation process is *classroom observation*, consisting of three components: planning, observation and feedback discussion. Appraisers are told to 'make observations throughout the school year – a minimum of four hours (including time to feed back).' In planning for observation they should, amongst other things:

> make certain that each teacher is aware that the observation of what happens in the classroom will be related both to overall performance and any pre-established targets.

Making the teacher so aware is likely to focus his/her attention on target attainment during the observed lessons. The guide suggests that during the feedback discussion a 'good observer' should:

- allow the teacher to talk
- check progress towards previously established targets
- focus on a limited number of areas (not more than three) for remedy/improvement/setting targets

- ensure careful recording so that commitments and suggestions to support improvements are not lost
- enable the teacher to diagnose his/her own performance and to suggest future needs and targets
- leave the teacher wanting to repeat the process.

In spite of the guidance that the feedback session should give the appraisee opportunities to talk and evaluate their own performance, it is clear that the discourse is framed by a particular conception of how good teaching should be appraised: namely, in terms of its instrumental effectiveness in achieving *pre-specified targets*. This conception is presumed to be non-problematic. The notes of guidance nowhere suggest that this view of good teaching is highly contestable. In other words the terms in which 'the discussion' is couched pre-empt the raising of certain issues about what constitutes good teaching.

Not only do the notes of guidance prescribe a feedback session which enables progress in attaining predetermined targets to be evaluated, but they also give the observer the role of suggesting further targets for the teacher to achieve. One function of these sessions then appears to be to keep the teachers' attention focused on targets to be achieved. This surely is also the point of asking observers to record their advice about how appraisees can improve their performance. Such advice would include targets to be aimed at and strategies for meeting them. In this way the appraiser can remind him/herself and the appraisee at some future point of the targets the latter should be aiming at.

Keeping the teacher's thinking focused on targets is also the point of keeping their number small. Having to think about many targets can result in a situation where the teacher is no longer able to focus his/her mind on any. However, focusing on only two or three targets, as recommended, encourages the teacher to regard teaching as a simple technical enterprise, rather than a complex practice whose specific elements need to be appraised in the light of the whole. Focusing attention continuously on a few targets is a good recipe for ensuring that the teacher is unable to 'see the wood for the trees'.

My interpretation of the Suffolk principles for observers is that they specify a form of control over the way teachers reflect and talk about their performance, while appearing to foster self-evaluation, dialogue and trust. If I am correct, then the view that good teaching consists solely of its instrumental effectiveness in achieving prespecified targets is an ideological construction which serves the purpose of hierarchically controlling performance.

The process outlined above constitutes a preparation for 'the appraisal dialogue' between appraiser and appraisee. The latter is described as a summative appraisal in the sense that it culminates in a formally recorded summary of a discussion about the appraisee's performance to date and of agreements reached concerning future targets and the training and support the appraisee needs to achieve them. The notes of guidance lists and defines the criteria the appraisal dialogue should satisfy. It must be objective, honest, constructive, valid, two-way, developmental, effective, realistic and encouraging. At a first glance few would disagree. The criteria as a whole appear to embrace a concern for both grounding judgements in factual evidence and giving positive guidance. However, 'objectivity' and 'honesty' are defined in ways which appear to rule out of the appraisal dialogue judgements which go beyond the facts of performance to focus on the personal qualities it manifests. It is implied that such judgements are inevitably conditioned or biased by the subjective values of the appraiser. The notes of guidance provide the following definitions of objectivity and honesty:

> Objective – by removing prejudice, subjective/unsubstantiated comment, and personality clashes.
>
> Honest – by giving the teacher an accurate picture of where he/she stands.

I would suggest some alternative definitions of these concepts:

> Honest – by making the personal biases and prejudices which underpin one's judgements clear to the teacher.
>
> Objective – being open to critiques of one's judgements by the teacher.

Embedded in these alternative sets of definitions are two quite different accounts of the object of appraisal. The first set encourages the appraiser to focus on the technical dimension of performance; on its instrumental effectiveness or consequences. Objective judgements of instrumental effectiveness are grounded entirely in factual evidence about the extent to which a course of action brings about its intended consequences (or targets). In the context of judging instrumental effectiveness objectively, an honest appraisal will be one in which the appraiser accurately represents the factual evidence of instrumental effectiveness, i.e. telling the appraisee where he/she stands in relation to his/her targets.

The criterial definitions of objectivity and honesty contained in the Suffolk guide presuppose that the appraisal dialogue is about the instrumental effectiveness of performance. It is in this context that one needs to locate the suggestions that the appraiser's role within the appraisal dialogue should be a positive one; constructive, effective, realistic. Since appraisals of instrumental effectiveness can be justified entirely by the facts about performance, such facts can also serve as a basis on which the appraiser can secure agreements about future courses of action. They legitimate this 'positive' role because they enable the appraiser to make 'constructive' and 'realistic' suggestions for improvements, based on evidence of 'strengths and past achievements', which the appraisee can accept.

The logic underpinning the criterial definitions of the appraiser's role in the appraisal interviews is as follows: by getting appraisees to see their performance from an instrumental point of view the appraiser is able to secure their agreement to a future plan of action. In other words the adoption of such a perspective by appraisees enables appraisers to control the outcome of the appraisal dialogue, and therefore the appraisee's future performance. The dialogue proceeds in a 'rational' sequence beginning, as the Suffolk guide advocates, 'with the appraisee's "self-appraisal"' and ending 'with a set of mutually agreed targets'. The initial 'self-appraisal', structured in terms of attainment targets, reinforces an instrumental view of practice, and thereby establishes the strong possibility that the appraisal dialogue will culminate in a consensus.

The alternative definitions of 'objectivity' and 'honesty', which I provided, presuppose a radically different perspective on teaching and its appraisal. They presuppose a value perspective which is expressed in judgments about the qualitative, rather than purely technical, aspects of performance. The qualitative dimension of teaching is manifested within the performance itself rather than its results. It constitutes the extent to which teachers realize or fail to realize in their interactions with students those values which define their professional identities as educators, e.g. care and respect for students as persons, a concern to protect and foster their powers of understanding and respect for their potential as self-actualizing and self-determining beings.

This view of teaching as a moral practice does not exclude the technical dimension but places it in a broader context of educational values. Appraisals of teaching are not viewed simply as judgements of instrumental effectiveness. They involve critiques of intended targets and/or the methods employed to achieve them, on the basis of perceived inconsistencies with the professional values and principles which constitute teaching as an *educational* process. Such critiques will inevitably be perceived by appraisees as threatening to some extent. They are not just critiques of performance but also of the professional 'self' or identity it manifests. Such critiques render a teacher's sense of self problematic.

This problem of identity is not necessarily resolved by an appeal to the facts. Such facts may be ambiguously interpreted because appraiser and appraisee disagree about what the professional values of teachers ought to be, or what constitutes evidence of their manifestation in practice. The appropriate context for handling such contestable appraisals is open and free dialogue in which appraiser and appraisee reflect together about their own and each other's interpretations of the facts and the evaluative perspectives embedded in them. In this context the concepts of 'objectivity' and 'honesty' take on rather different meanings to the ones they possess in the context of purely technical dialogue. Moreover, such dialogue need not result in total agreement. Both appraiser and appraisee may emerge from it having modified and changed their views. Through it they may both develop their personal understanding of professional values, and what constitutes a realization of them in practice, but still 'beg to differ' in some respects. It would be quite inappropriate for the appraiser to attempt to secure agreement to a future plan of action. Moral dialogue about teaching, when genuine, gives the teacher the right to self-determine his/her own future practice.

Genuine moral dialogue keeps the threat experienced by moral appraisals of teaching to a level which stimulates but does not inhibit self-reflection. But it is quite inconsistent with a hierarchical relation between appraiser and appraisee. When moral appraisals are hierarchically structured, the level of threat is inevitably high. The existence of the hierarchical relation symbolizes the uncontestable moral authority of the appraiser.

In an earlier document (1986) Suffolk Education Department advised that appraisal should not involve inferences about the personal qualities manifested in performance. This policy is not simply about reassuring teachers. The trade-off it secures is to reduce the threat and anxiety hierarchical appraisal arouses in teachers in exchange for getting them to accept purely instrumental conceptions of their practices.

The policy of ruling out inferences about the personal qualities of teachers constitutes a mechanism of 'ideology formation' because it focuses attention on quantifiable performance targets. According to Suffolk's practical guide, targets should 'be stated in clear, unambiguous language; be few in number . . . ; be measurable or observable.' This 'target ideology' facilitates hierarchical control over the performances of teachers. The targets are largely derived from 'the job description', and department, school and LEA policies. They are hierarchically imposed, rather than self-generated within a framework of of professional values. The alternative way of reducing the threat and anxiety of appraisal is to construe it as a form of unsequenced moral discourse between professional peers which enables each person to develop capacities (e.g. of reflexivity) for self-determining improvements in the quality of their teaching.

The final phase of the appraisal process outlined by Suffolk is the monitoring of the appraiser's 'help and support' by the appraisee's 'grandparent'; a procedure which reinforces hierarchical control over the latter's thinking and performance.

The Suffolk appraisal process poses the danger of alienating the professional self of a teacher from his/her performance. If successful, teaching will lack 'soul' because the teacher will lose touch with him/herself. Teacher development then becomes a process of acquiring low-level technical/instrumental skills, in contrast to a process of developing the professional wisdom to realize educational values in concrete forms of action. Competence gets defined as a mastery of techniques rather than a mastery of the self in the service of the professional values it professes. The teacher becomes deprofessionalized and transformed into a technician, thereby losing a professional identity which has been defined by the values of the professional culture.

Teacher appraisal as outlined in the Suffolk guide can be interpreted as an attack on the professional culture, since it isolates the individual teacher from the influence of peers by bringing his/her performance under the direct surveillance and control of a 'line manager'. In this way discourse about practice is hierarchalized, and institutionalized opportunities for lateral communication and the sharing of experience between peers restricted. The development of a distinctive professional culture is jeopardized. Claims by teachers to have a special knowledge and understanding of the aims and processes of education get interpreted as rationalizations for 'restrictive practices' which are inconsistent with providing an efficient service to the consumers of education.

Appraisal of the kind I have described can be viewed as part of a broader political strategy to transform the cultures of social organizations which have previously provided a buffer, a social space between individuals and the state. Nicholas Boyle (1988) has argued that such autonomous or semi-autonomous organizations have protected individuals from direct state interference and given 'shape and substance and continuity to their lives, a focus for loyalty and a place of engagement with other citizens that is not simply an extension of the market-place . . .' Boyle suggests that the most significant of all these attacks on intermediate organizations has been our present government's assault on the professions:

> The case of the professions is significant because it shows that Thatcherism is indeed hostile to the whole range of social institutions that are not part of the state, and not simply to those that exercise quasi-government functions. A profession is by definition a corporation that restricts its membership by other than market considerations, and professional standards are standards imposed not by the market but by the opinion of fellow-professionals. You cannot have professional standards without professional restrictive practices and an assault on restrictive practices is an assault on the professional institutions themselves.

He goes on to conclude that:

> There is no room in the Thatcherite view for any social units larger than the individual, and the individual has his identity only as a unit of consumption or of labour, not as one who shares in the life of any institution . . .
>
> . . . in a consumer society people's labour is expensive. This, however, does not mean that in it people themselves are of worth . . . Like expensive computing time, people must be used to the full when switched on and be either instantly transferable to another function when one job is completed or else simply switched off. In the language of Thatcherism: people – that is workers – must be flexible, or unemployed . . . They are in short to be dismembered, reduced to a series of functions that they exercise in accordance with no principle of continuity of their own choosing but only with the demands of the market.

One could view the Suffolk practical guide to appraisal as a micropolitical strategy for penetrating the professional culture and subordinating those elements which restrict the utility of individuals as marketable commodities. In this view it constitutes a device for reducing the individual teacher to a flexible resource in the labour market: one with an infinitely plastic and malleable nature, capable of being remoulded in whatever shape is required. Within the Suffolk scheme performance targets can be continuously redefined in the light of changing job descriptions and LEA, school and departmental policies. Appraisal can then be used as a device for rationalizing the acquisition and distribution of marketable skills. Redeployment does not have to be made explicit as a function of appraisal. The possibility of using appraisal in this way is implicit in the very form and structure of the process outlined in the practical guide; one which embodies the assumption that 'professional development' is the individualistic and possessive process of acquiring techniques.

Appraisal, as advocated in the Suffolk guide, is not simply a strategy which operates on the professional soul of the teacher. It is also a strategy which operates on the soul of the manager. Within an autonomous professional organization managers are professional leaders. Their task is to regulate, orchestrate and co-ordinate the activities of individuals so that they realize shared professional goals, values and standards. But within an overall assault on intermediate organizations by the state, managers are pressurized into detaching themselves from the professional culture to become agents of state control at the workface. Teacher-appraisal schemes which construct an ideology of teaching also construct an ideology of school management which legitimates it as an agency of state control.

The Suffolk guide should not be viewed as an idiosyncratic interpretation of the criteria established in national agreements. Hewton (1988) in a state-of-play review of the national scene suggests that the general trend is to embrace 'a "top down" form of appraisal involving interviews conducted by a senior person – either a headteacher, deputy head or head of department.' He refers to alternative approaches which have evolved organically in some schools outside the process of national policy development. They 'relate to self-evaluation and peer appraisal (as distinct from line management appraisal)', but Hewton concludes that 'it is unlikely these will play a major part in any widely adopted scheme.' Schemes of appraisal currently being devised in some universities also appear to be taking a similar hierarchical shape. The use of appraisal as a management tool seems to be an immovable force.

Is a counter-hegemonic practice of appraisal possible?

Outside the context of the national pilot schemes many LEAs have, in spite of some initial and I believe misguided pressure from the teachers' unions, proceeded with the development of appraisal schemes in their schools. Some LEAs did so with the quite explicit intention of supporting the organic development of appraisal schemes from the grassroots. Their hope was that these can then be accommodated to any extensions of the ACAS criteria resulting from the national pilot schemes. Such LEAs were aware that the government might wish to establish standardized procedures and strategies nationally, rather than allow variation within a criterial framework which was open to ambiguous interpretations. In which case overt conflict would emerge between national and some local appraisal policies. However, the hope was that only an amended criterial framework would be established.

Those LEAs fostering 'bottom up' development can be viewed as facilitating a counter-hegemonic strategy. But it is not simply an 'oppositional' one. Rather it is an exercise in creative conformity; a strategy for securing a form of appraisal which genuinely fosters *professional* development, yet at the same time appears to conform to the nationally negotiated rhetoric. Some of these 'counter-hegemonic' LEAs are now in a postion to observe some of the developments they have initiated coming to fruition and may be grateful that they were not invited to participate in the national pilots. The latter involves the implementation of schemes which tended to be bureaucratically constructed in the light of the ACAS criteria. Developments in some LEAs outside the national pilots have emerged from official support for the dissemination, comparison and discussion amongst the teaching profession of school-initiated schemes. In at least one of these LEAs a 'creative compromise' is emerging between peer- and management-based appraisal. The London Borough of Enfield is evolving a two-tier model.

Earlier I suggested that something like a two-tier model was implicit in the NUT's reservations about ambiguities in the ACAS agreement. Indeed in one earlier paper (see Elliott 1988a) I attempted to articulate this model in a more explicit form, using teacher-based action research as the paradigm for the first-tier peer appraisal.

Teacher-based action research can be characterized as follows:

1 It focuses on the identification, clarification and resolution of problems teachers face in realizing their educational values in practice. As a form of inquiry it is a practical/moral rather than theoretical/technical science.
2 It involves joint reflection on means and ends. Educational values as ends are defined by the concrete actions a teacher selects as the means of realizing them. Such values are realized in a teacher's interactions with students and not as an extrinsic outcome of them. Teaching activities constitute practical interpretations of values. Therefore in reflecting about the quality of his/her teaching a teacher must reflect about the concepts of value which shape and give it form.
3 It is a reflexive practice. As a form of self-evaluation or self-appraisal, action research is not simply a matter of the teacher evaluating his/her actions from any perspective, e.g. that of their technical effectiveness. It is primarily a matter of the teacher evaluating the qualities of his/her 'self' as they are

manifested in actions. From this perspective such actions are conceived as moral practices rather than mere expressions of techniques. Self-appraisal in the context of a moral practice involves a particular type of self-reflection; namely, reflexivity.

4 It integrates theory into practice. *Educational* theories are viewed as systems of values, ideas and beliefs which are represented not so much in a propositional form, as in a form of practice. Such theories are developed by reflectively improving practice. Theory development and the improvement of practice are not viewed as separate processes.

5 It involves dialogue with professional peers. Inasmuch as teachers strive through action research to realize professional values in action, they are accountable for the outcome to their professional peers. Such accountability is expressed in the production of records which document changes in practice and the processes of deliberation/reflection through which they were brought about.

Whitehead (1989) has argued that such records tacitly imply a teacher's claim to self-understanding, i.e. to know his/her own professional development. Such a claim constitutes an invitation to peers to engage in a professional dialogue about the validity of a teacher's practical interpretations of educational values as these are evidenced in the records provided. This kind of dialogue can influence a teacher's self-understanding and stimulate new direction for practical inquiry. Self-appraisal and peer-appraisal are both integral to educational action research.

The process I have described above is barely accommodated within the kind of management-led appraisal illustrated in the Suffolk practical guide. The peer appraisal is distorted by being individualized and hierarchalized in the form of the formal appraisal interview. Accountability is exercised upwards to a line-manager rather than laterally to a professional peer-group. I have already demonstrated how the discourse of the hierarchical formal interview is structured in a manner which rules out the kind of free and open dialogue cited in 5, and by implication the conception of teaching as a moral practice that such dialogue rests on. In focusing attention on the instrumental effectiveness of actions, the discourse structure of the hierarchical interview encourages teachers to dissociate their actions from the educational values which define their identities as professionals. The appraisal interview permits reflection on the technical aspects of performance but not a reflexivity in which teachers evaluate their actions as manifestations of 'self' in the light of the educational values they profess.

Now, of course, it can be argued that discourse about targets can refer as much to values as to concrete objectives. Why, for example, cannot a commitment to the value of fostering co-operative learning be defined in terms of tangible targets. The answer is quite simple. To do so would be to distort and inhibit the development of a teacher's understanding of what it means to foster co-operative learning. Such an understanding can never be finally fixed. It develops and evolves through continuing reflection by a teacher about the strategies (s)he adopts to foster co-operative learning in a range and variety of contexts. To define strategies operationally for fostering co-operative learning in the form of fixed targets is to pre-empt the kind of reflective process described in 3.

It is not only the peer appraisal which is distorted by the structure of discourse in the hierarchical formal appraisal interview. The meaning of self-appraisal is distorted by focusing attention on the technical aspects of teaching and neglecting the moral aspects. This happens not only within the interview itself. The value of the earlier self-appraisal and classroom observation phases is construed purely in instrumental terms: as a preparation for the appraisal interview rather than as a worthwhile professional development process in itself. The result is that these phases are also individualized and hierarchalized. The self-appraising teacher reflects in isolation from his/her professional peers, and in the light of a hierarchically constructed agenda of questions. The questions for self-appraisal are not self-constructed. Similarly, classroom observation is not a reciprocal arrangement between peers but a hierarchically managed procedure.

A two-tier model of appraisal, in which action research constitutes a first-tier process, would prevent self and peer appraisals being distorted by the individualization and hierarchalization which results from their subordination to the formal appraisal interview. The first tier would constitute a process of professional development in itself, capable of enabling individuals to identify their own learning needs and of determining how these are best provided for. Indeed it would be a major task of management to facilitate and support such an action-research process at the organizational level, e.g. with respect to the provision of time for reflection, peer observation and teachers' meetings.

However, the two-tier model also acknowledges the legitimate appraisal functions of management. The latter need to monitor the extent to which the first-tier process is enabling the professional development of staff, and they need to assess the potential contribution of individuals to roles and tasks within the organization. The records constructed by individuals and 'validated' in dialogue with peers during the course of the first-tier process of action research would constitute the data base for a management-led appraisal of how individual potentials might be developed and used to the benefit of the institution. Such records would incorporate accounts of the validating dialogue with peers, in which areas of agreement and disagreement were documented. Within this two-tier model, the individual teacher in discussion with peers would select and organize the material for the formal appraisal interview. Access of managers to performance data would therefore be controlled by appraisees and their peers, and release of data would depend upon the confidence and trust the latter were able to establish with the former. Part of this would involve establishing agreements about the conditions governing access to the second-tier appraisal records beyond the boundaries of the institution.

The advantage of the two-tier model is that it limits the use of teacher appraisal to management functions which can easily be legitimated to professionals in educational institutions. The formal interview can provide an opportunity for managers to engage in genuine two-way dialogue with those at 'the chalk-face' about how the organization can both meet professional needs and support the development of demonstrated potential.

At least one LEA, the London Borough of Enfield, has been encouraging its teachers to discuss the possibility of developing this two-tier model in schools (see Boothroyd and Burbidge 1988). This is partly due to my own involvement as a consultant for Enfield on teacher appraisal. But it is also due to the fact that one of the first schools in Enfield to evolve its own appraisal scheme organically appeared to do so along two-tier lines. Boothroyd and Burbidge, two senior teachers released from their schools to stimulate reflection about appraisal in the teaching force, case-studied this school and argue that its development of a two-strand model was an example of 'the removal of threat by creating ownership'. They claim that:

> The staff were concerned that the appraisal should not be done by one person, and that observation of lessons would pose a potential threat. Through consultation and staff discussion a model of peer group observation was developed.

There is some evidence that the bottom-up development of two-tier schemes in response to the threat of managerial models – which individualize, hierarchalize and technologize appraisal processes – is not an isolated event. Reports of such schemes, from those responsible for monitoring developments in LEAs which have opted for organic development, are on the increase. The growth of such schemes can be explained in terms of the professional culture's response to the managerial hegemony expressed in many of the national pilot schemes.

Two-tier approaches constitute, as Boothroyd and Burbidge claim, a strategy for removing threat by creating ownership. They constitute what I have termed a *creative compromise* between the prevailing professional culture and the growth of management in educational institutions. Such a compromise is more than a mere accommodation to elements of an invading culture, as the development of individualized, hierarchalized and technologized approaches like the Suffolk scheme appear to be. Such approaches do indeed embrace certain features of the dominant professional culture of teachers. The incorporation of the classroom observation element, for example, reflects the priority teachers give to work in classrooms with students; their feeling that professional acknowledgements and rewards should be largely based on appraisals of such work, and that in-service training resources should largely be directed to helping them function better in classrooms. But these accommodations do not prevent appraisal from being used as a device for ideologically reconstructing the culture of teachers, so that they come to view their performance in classrooms in ways which legitimate the hegemony of the state. The creative component in the two-tier approach is that it not only weakens this hegemony but also establishes new conditions for the development of the professional culture.

The traditional culture of teachers has largely taken the form of craft knowledge: 'know-how' encapsulated in behavioural repertoires which are transmitted as common-sense tips within the professional peer group and fine-tuned in trial-and-error experience of numerous classroom settings. The craft knowledge, embodied in the behavioural repertoires experienced teachers draw on, is largely treated as a matter of common sense. The values, ideas and beliefs which underpin it are not in the main objects of conscious reflection. The craft culture does not necessarily entail reflexive practice.

The growth of the educational action-research movement within the UK over the past 25 years marks a transformation from the traditional craft culture to a reflective culture in which teaching strategies are perceived as potentially problematic and therefore objects of reflective deliberation in particular contexts. Within a reflective professional culture teaching strategies are treated as provisional, context-dependent and hypothetical. Such a culture also generates analytic frameworks which enable teachers to anticipate the problems and issues particular strategies may pose with respect to the realization of educational aims and values.

It may well be the case that the organic development of two-tier approaches to teacher appraisal in schools is drawing on the legacy of the action-research movement which first evolved during the 1960s in the UK during the period of widespread curriculum reform. The impact of such action-research programmes on the development of the professional culture of teachers within the UK has yet to be systematically evaluated.

It is significant that the action-research movement emerged as the pace of social change rendered the traditional craft practices of teachers problematic. In other words, it is only when social change renders the common-sense wisdom of the craft culture problematic that teachers experience a need to engage in deliberative reflection about their educational values and how best to realize them in practice.

However, an additional stimulus to the development of a reflective professional culture in the late 60s and early 70s was the threat of increasing political control over educational practices in schools. The threat was manifested in early attempts to establish, through curriculum-reform projects at the national level, sets of behaviourally defined learning outcomes. Stenhouse explicitly resisted accommodating the specification of behavioural objectives within the Humanities Project and generated an oppositional 'process model' of curriculum development as the basis for the project's design (see Stenhouse 1975). This process model was characterized by a specification of a teaching–learning process in terms of educational values which it was the task of teachers to realize reflectively in their practices. At the heart of the process model stood the teacher as a researcher. The experience of the threat of political/ administrative regulation over the practices of teachers was indeed part of the conditions which stimulated the emergence of the action-research movement in the UK over 25 years ago.

Although the emergence of counter-hegemonic two-tier appraisal schemes from the grassroots may owe a great deal to the impact of the educational action-research movement on the professional culture, we must also view such schemes as indications of the further growth and development of a reflective and critical professional culture. The threat of a managerially transmitted hegemony in the form of teacher appraisal has itself established a condition which stimulates the further growth of action research as a central feature of the professional culture of teachers. The threat, although real, opens up creative possibilities for the transformation of this culture. Two-tier schemes grounded in action research illustrate such possibilities. They are not simply strategies of resistance which accommodate a degree of compromise. The resistance takes the form of a very creative compromise indeed.

Foucault (1980) has argued that:

There are no relations of power without resistances; the latter are all the more real and effective because they are formed right at the point where relations of power are exercised; resistance to power does not have to come from elsewhere to be real, nor is it inexorably frustrated through being the compatriot of power. It exists all the more by being in the same place as power; hence, like power, resistance is multiple and can be integrated in global strategies.

In his book *Theory and Resistance in Education* (1983) Giroux argues that Foucault's analysis of power relations reminds us that they are never uni-dimensional. Power expressed as domination is countered by power expressed as resistance. According to Giroux we lack an adequate account of resistance to the hegemony of the state in educational institutions, and he warns us against equating resistance with any form of oppositional behaviour. The former has a creative and productive dimension which the latter may lack. He claims that:

inherent in a radical notion of resistance is an expressed hope, an element of transcendence, for radical transformation – a notion that appears to be missing from a number of radical theories of education that appear trapped in the theoretical cemetery of Orwellian pessimism.

The theories he refers to are those based on an interpretation of Marx which implies that social practices are determined by and reproduce the prevailing power relations within society. Such theories view teachers and schools as passive vehicles of social reproduction. Giroux argues that as a theoretical construct the idea of resistance points to a need to:

> Understand more thoroughly the complex ways in which people mediate and respond to the interface between their own lived experiences and structures of domination and constraint.

The study of the emergence of two-tier schemes of teacher appraisal may indeed give us a keener appreciation of how the lived experience of teachers in classrooms and schools interacts with structures of domination enforced by the agencies of the state.

I would suggest that it is a mistake to view the professional culture of teachers and the values, ideas and beliefs of which it consists solely as ideological structures which shape practice and legitimate its subordination to the purposes of the state. Such a view, expressed by many radical educational theorists, adopts what Block (1985) calls an anthropological theory of cognition. This theory, partly derived from Durkheim, asserts that our everyday practices are determined by cognitive structures which are derived from history and tradition rather than experience. These historically transmitted collective representations of reality (cultures) are then defined as ideologics, or misrepresentations of reality, by incorporating Marx's explanation of certain cognitive structures as legitimating relations of domination and thereby preventing people from becoming aware of their real interests.

Block points out that anthropologists, and others who draw on their ideological theory of cognition, have forgotten that in the *German Ideology* Marx discussed two types of processes in the formation of everyday practical knowledge. He argued that some aspects of cognition were the products of interaction with the environment and other people. According to Block this latter type of explanation is very similar to 'the well-documented conclusion of modern developmental psychologists that the child forms concepts as the result of a pre-linguistic analytic process on the basis of interactions with the environment.' In other words, 'a child is not taught categories or modes of reasoning but *constructs* them from his experience . . .' Block concludes that such a well-documented finding of developmental psychologists 'rules out the view that cognition is an arbitrary scheme developed outside practical experience and learned ready-made from elders and betters . . .' Everyday practical knowledge, according to Block, is not all of a kind but the outcome of 'at least two fundamentally different processes': namely, the transmission of misrepresentations of reality which legitimate relations of exploitation and domination, and the construction of representations on the basis of interaction with the natural and social environment. The latter is the primary process. The process for transmitting ideologies depends on common-sense knowledge which is developed through interaction with the natural and social environment. Ideology affirms and negates common-sense knowledge. Block argues that this is how 'ideology can mystify, invert and hide the real conditions of existence.' I have argued in this paper that some teacher-appraisal schemes operate to transmit and sustain misrepresentations of teaching. They do this by distorting representations of teaching which emerge from the practical experience of encountering students in classrooms.

Teaching involves influencing students in a manner which enables them to learn. It is therefore experienced as an activity directed towards an end. But encounters with students generate conceptions of moral obligation to them in their capacity as learners. It is from such interpersonal encounters that teachers construct both the concept of learning as their end in view and the concepts of value which guide the means they employ in realizing it. This experience of teaching as a moral enterprise (see Elliott 1989a) is both affirmed and negated when teachers are manipulated into adopting an instrumental view of their activity. Such a view holds that the end of teaching is learning and that it is a source of moral obligation. In this way the instrumental ideology affirms aspects of a teacher's practical experience. But it also negates that experience in viewing learning as a product of the teacher's activity rather than an enabling activity which is constituted as such by its ethical qualities. Within the framework of an ideology which separates conceptions of ends from conceptions of means, ethical obligations become displaced. They become associated with a teacher's commitment to producing quantifiable end-states in students, rather than with a commitment to realizing certain qualities in his/her interactions with them as learners.

I would argue that there are limits on the extent to which educational practices can simply reproduce an instrumental ideology which legitimates the hegemony of the state. These limits are experienced in the everyday encounters that teachers have with their students and manifest themselves as problems within those encounters. Such problems may not be consciously articulated but experienced as feelings of irritation, frustration and anger which arise when students demonstrate an unwillingness to be treated as infinitely plastic and malleable material which can be moulded into any desired shape the system requires. These feelings may also be accompanied by feelings of guilt. For there is a sense in which the teacher 'knows' what (s)he is doing: namely, transcending certain ethical limits in his/her pedagogical relation with students. This experience of dilemmas within the pedagogical relation arises from a tension within the self-understanding of the teacher, between its ideologically structured elements and those elements which (s)he has constructed on the basis of classroom experience.

The professional cultures of teachers constitute resources of knowledge they draw on for interpreting classroom situations and making decisions within them. Their practices cannot be explained solely in terms of the reproduction of ideologically structured knowledge. Professional cultures will include ideological elements but also ways of understanding which evolve on the basis of teachers' experience of pedagogical environments. As pedagogical environments change over time, these ways of understanding are continuously reconstructed. Professional cultures are not static but dynamic practical traditions continuously reconstructed by teachers on the basis of experience.

This interaction between professional cultures and practical experience often occurs below the level of conscious self-reflection. The acquisition and utilization of professional knowledge is a largely tacit and intuitive process. It is only when teachers experience severe dilemmas which arise from conflicting elements in their self-understanding of what they are doing that they are prompted into conscious self-reflection. The emergence of a reflective practice is both a critical and creative enterprise. It is critical because it involves a critique of the ideologically distorted components of teachers' self-understandings in the light of their reflections upon experience. It is creative because, in attempting to resolve dilemmas in their self-understandings, teachers develop new ways of understanding the relationship between educational values and their practices. On the basis of my experience as a facilitator of educational action research in schools and classrooms I would assert that this self-reflective process always involves teachers in clarifying the nature of the dilemmas evidenced in their practices and the ambiguous self-understandings they manifest.

The emergence of action research within a two-tier model of appraisal is a response to both an internal and external threat, and the two are not unconnected. The internal threat implicit in the experience of dilemmas is to the values which define the professional identities of teachers as educators; identities established in numerous encounters with students in classrooms. Feelings of being threatened stem from the pressure on teachers to reproduce ideological conceptions of practice which legitimate the hegemony of the state. This is why the imposition of a hierarchized appraisal scheme is experienced as a threat. Such a scheme reinforces the ideological components in teachers' practices and thereby enhances the dilemmas experienced by the 'educational self'. The connection, between the threat of formal appraisal schemes and the dilemmas teachers experience in their everyday interactions with students, explains why the former can stimulate the growth of educational action research in schools as a form of resistance to ideological hegemony. The growth of school-based action research as a form of ideological resistance expressed in two-tier schemes of appraisal implies that the source of resistance to the hegemony of the state lies in teachers' own self-understandings of their practices; in the ambiguities and tensions implicit in them.

There is a dangerous account of action research currently being perpetuated by certain radical theorists who have been influenced by the critical theory of Jurgen Habermas (see McCarthy 1978). Such theorists have tended to perpetuate an assumption contained in the anthropological theory of cognition: namely, that the self-understandings teachers have of their everyday practices constitute ideologically distorted misrepresentations of reality. Therefore a critique of ideology must come from understandings generated by a critical social science. It is the task of such a science to provide teachers with critical

theorems which explain how their self-understandings misrepresent teaching
and learning processes and legitimate hegemony.

Of course, all this involves a dialogue between the critical educational
theorist and teachers, since a critical theory can only be validated in teachers'
own self-understandings as it prompts them to reflect upon their experience of
classrooms and schools. Nevertheless, action research tends to be portrayed as
a process which depends on an external source for theory generation.
Teachers' self-understandings of their practices, unassisted by a critical social
science, cannot constitute the source of an ideology critique, since they are
themselves products of ideological conditioning. It follows that teachers'
self-understandings cannot alone serve as the basis for their emancipation
from ideological control. Teachers need to be emancipated through interaction with the critical theorems of the educational scientist.

This position tends to permeate, sometimes ambiguously, what has now
become a major source of action-research theory: Carr and Kemmis' *Becoming
Critical: Knowing through Action Research* (1983). The dominance of the
anthropological theory of cognition in this work is illustrated by the following
passages in which the authors are commenting on, and apparently endorsing,
Habermas's conception of critical theory:

> any reduction of the social sciences to the explication of subjective
> meanings ['self-understandings': my brackets] fails to recognize that the
> subjective meanings that characterize social life are themselves con-
> ditioned by an objective context that limits both the scope of individuals'
> intentions and the possibility of their realization.

> emancipatory interest requires going beyond any narrow concerns with
> subjective meaning in order to acquire an emancipatory knowledge of
> the objective framework within which communication and social action
> occur. It is with this emancipatory knowledge that a critical social science
> is essentially concerned.

> if, as Habarmas concedes, self-reflection and self-understanding may be
> distorted by social conditions, then the rational capabilities of human
> beings for self-emancipation will only be realized if critical theory can
> elucidate these conditions and reveal how they can be eliminated.

> The *Verstehen* method ['eliciting subjective understandings': my
> brackets] is insufficient ... because it provides no critical basis for
> rendering the nature of social life problematic.

All of the passages appear to deny the possibility that teachers' self-
understandings of their practices can alone constitute a source of critical
self-reflection and emancipatory action. The authors neglect the ambiguities,
conflicts and tensions contained within these self-understandings and therefore do not seriously entertain the possibility of a self-generating, reflexive and
critical pedagogy emerging as a form of action research. It is a possibility which

renders false the distinction Carr and Kemmis draw between a 'practical' and 'emancipatory' paradigm of action research.

I have argued, to the contrary, that a self-generating critical pedagogy is possible as a form of creative resistance to the hegemony of the state, and that it is evidenced in the emergence of two-tier approaches to teacher appraisal. A detailed study of such approaches may well advance our understanding of how the power of the state interacts with the professional culture of teachers.

8

Competency-based training and the education of the professions: is a happy marriage possible?

This chapter looks at yet another emerging government initiative; namely, competency-based education for the professions. The author critiques the behaviourist model of competency-based training and suggests that a quality assurance/control system need not depend on it. He develops an alternative framework and methodology for describing quality in professional activities like teaching, and indicates how action research can form the basis of a non-behaviourist form of competency-based teacher education.

In this chapter I shall attempt to reconstruct the ideas of competency-based education/training and assessment drawing on:

(a) an alternative conceptualization of competence.
(b) a stage model depicting its development.
(c) an alternative methodology for identifying the abilities which characterize it.

In doing so, I shall try to generate an alternative account of *quality control* or *assurance* which resolves the now familiar dilemma between *accountability* and *self-determined professional development*. Although my major concern will be with the education of the teaching profession, the general argument is relevant to quality-control issues being currently debated amongst a variety of professional groups and those responsible for their education and training.

Stated quite simply, the situation is that a lot of individuals who see themselves as professionals do not like the competency-based approach to appraisal, training and job selection in their occupation. They are told that it will deliver quality. They believe that it will deliver managerial control over their performance, leave less room for professional judgement and reduce their status to that of a technical operative. The CBTE approach appears to deny any validity to the professional knowledge they have acquired from their professional education, and perhaps even more importantly, from years of direct hands-on experience.

The educators of professionals in higher education are often not too happy with this form of 'quality assurance' either. It appears to deny a substantial role for theoretical understanding as a basis for professional practice, and therefore marginalizes the contribution of academic institutions to the development of the professions.

In my own professional area of teaching, school teachers tend to dislike the idea of appraisal, particularly when it is suggested that national performance criteria can be defined as a basis for publicly identifying the bad eggs and rewarding the good ones. The response to any such suggestion is that 'good teaching' cannot be defined, at least on any agreed basis. Its indefinable qualities, however, may be intuitively discerned by experienced and trusted peers. There is now a measure of acceptance for a national scheme based on the intuitive appraisals of senior professional peers, in which the appraisal record will remain largely confidential.

In higher education some teacher educators, like myself, have been mounting innovatory professional development programmes which reject a theory-applying model of educational practice and embrace the idea of teachers as action researchers or reflective practitioners capable of determining their own performance on the basis of self-reflection. CBET appears to be inconsistent with this rapidly emerging approach in higher education to the education and training of teachers.

Quality assurance and the search for fundamentals

The widespread emergence of *fundamentalism* in the late 20th century is not confined to religious traditions. It is evidenced in most of the 'reforms' now sweeping our social institutions, including those of education and training. The competency-based education and training movement is one example.

Fundamentalist movements generally possess four key characteristics. First, they attempt to reduce social practices to a small number of essential elements, against which the practices as a whole can be judged. Their view of standards is an atomistic one. Competence is specified as a number of discrete, atomized abilities which are held to represent its essential elements. Second, the essentials are derived from what is held to be an indubitable foundation of knowledge, such as the Bible or, in the case of the competency movement, a science of management concerned with the prediction and control of human behaviour. As the Bible offers the assurance of salvation, so management science offers educational administrators an assurance of quality in an educational process conceived as a mode of production. Johnson (1984), in an historical analysis of the quest for the competent teacher, interestingly locates the rise of management science in what he calls the 'messianic industrialism' of post-war America.

Third, the essential elements of the fundamentalist's credo must refer to concrete tangible and measurable phenomena. Christ's resurrection and virgin birth are considered by Christian fundamentalists to be concrete events in time and place rather than symbolic meanings people construct to make sense of their lives. Similarly 'competencies' were viewed within the competency-based teacher education (CBTE) movement of the 70s in the USA as concrete, tangible and measurable components of teacher behaviour. Fourth, the essential elements are viewed as unchanging rather than culturally and socially relative. They are neither socially constructed nor historically conditioned. Just as the laws of God revealed in the Bible are valid irrespective of the reader's location in time and place, so the findings of management science can reveal the unchanging laws governing the production of learning in classrooms. According to Johnson, such was the quest of E. L. Thorndike, whom he describes as the pedagogical midwife of 'messianic industrialism' in American education, and of all those educational researchers who followed him in attempting to measure the 'component ability atoms' involved in the process of educational production.

Fundamentalist movements always emerge to purify social institutions from 'contaminating' influences, usually some form of liberalism. Thus CBTE emerged in the USA to purify teachers of the liberal-humanist educational theories promoted by their teacher educators and held to be responsible for the attitudes of the permissive society and its attendant evils. The reduction of teaching to its essential behavioural components offered the prospect of a high degree of prediction and control over teachers' future conduct, thereby eliminating the contaminating influence of liberal-humanist educational theory.

Doll (1984) argues that the competency-based education movement was on the wane in the USA. Indeed he prefers to write about it in the past tense. 'Messianic industrialism' and its CBET progeny appear to have been exported to the UK during the late 80s. Whereas, in the USA the CBET movement originated in teacher education (see Tuxworth 1989), this area has yet to be colonized in the UK. The prospective 'colonizers' are the National Council for Vocational Qualifications (NCVQ). They recently funded a conference on CBET in higher education and are currently involved in some pilot teacher-education projects with LEAs. One possible future scenario is the accreditation of teacher in-service by the NCVQ, enabling LEAs to bypass higher-education institutions which fail to come into line with the CBET model of quality assurance.

The NCVQ was established in 1987 following the publication of the government White Paper *Working Together – Education and Training* (1985). In 1988 the Manpower Services Commission (the forerunner of the Training Agency (TA)) published a series of guidance notes on 'The development of assessable standards for national certification'. Guidance Note 3 on *The Definition of Competence and Performance Criteria* locates the NCVQ model firmly in the US CBET tradition.

A competence is a description of something which a person who works in a given occupational area should be able to do. It is a description of an action, behaviour, or outcome which the person should be able to demonstrate.

Performance criteria are statements by which an assessor judges the evidence that an individual can perform the activity specified in the competence, to a level acceptable in employment.

An element of competence describes what can be done; an action, behaviour or outcome which a person should be able to demonstrate. Or an element of competence may describe such things as the knowledge or understanding which is essential if performance is to be sustained, or extended to new situations within the occupation.

A unit of competence will be made up of a number of elements (together with associated performance criteria) which together make sense to, and are valued by, employers so that they warrant separate accreditation. Vocational qualifications will normally be made up of a number of related units which together will comprise a statement of competence relevant to an occupation.

An underlying concern with prediction and control in the language employed is quite clear, as indeed is the atomistic approach to competency specification. The model has been blessed by the Confederation of British Industry (CBI) Task Force on Training in its report *Towards a Skills Revolution – a Youth Charter* (see Jessup 1989).

Towards an alternative model of quality assurance through competency-based education and training

The NCVQ and Department of Employment are currently attempting to accommodate criticisms of their model on the grounds that it neglects the educational and personal development aspects of training. Alison Wolf (1989) argues that there is 'no bifurcation between competence and education' in the sense that knowledge is central to the latter but not the former. She claims that knowledge and understanding in here in any competence and can therefore be directly inferred from the performance in which any given competence is demonstrated. This includes general as well as context-specific knowledge since the latter is embedded in general structures of knowledge. To learn something specific is also to learn something in general, argues Wolf. Therefore general knowledge structures may best be developed in their context of use rather than in decontextualized form. CBET is therefore not necessarily anti-educational. If performances are outputs of competence, Wolf argues, then knowledge and understanding are inputs. All of which, she has pointed out, is perfectly compatible with NCVQ's account of knowledge and understanding as 'underpinning performance (and competence).'

The critics of CBET may not be entirely happy with this accommodation of the educational perspective. They may reject the assumption that all forms of knowledge and understanding have only an instrumental value, as a source of technical rules for accomplishing tasks effectively.

Pearson (1984) draws a distinction between 'habitual skill knowledge' and 'intelligent skill knowledge' and argues that only the former can be derived directly from an analysis of tasks an occupant of a role is required to perform. The acquisition of habitual skill knowledge enables a person to perform unreflectively certain necessary routines. According to Pearson such technical know-how is a necessary but not sufficient condition of competence. Thus one would not deem a car driver competent solely on the grounds that s(he) knew how to start up, move, stop, etc. The driver might have the appropriate habitual skill knowledge and create havoc and chaos on the roads. In which case s(he) would be judged an incompetent driver. In order to be judged competent the driver would have to display situational understanding. It is the abilities exercised in this respect that Pearson calls 'intelligent skill knowledge'. It involves the exercise of capacities for discernment, discrimination and intelligent action. It is only by exercising these capacities that a car driver can avoid creating havoc on the roads and thereby endangering the safety of others.

Pearson argues that the behaviourist ideology which has underpinned the CBET movement has resulted in misconceived attempts to reduce intelligent skill knowledge to a form of habitual skill knowledge. Indeed, a recent example of such reductionism in the UK context is Wolf's (1989) paper on the Knowledge/Competence issue. She assumes that the assessment of high-level cognitive functioning can be accommodated within the NCVQ model, so that what constitutes evidence of such functioning can be specified in terms of performance criteria. In other words, such functioning will manifest itself in terms of predictable performance outcomes. Pearson claims the opposite. In attributing competence to individuals across a whole range of practices which call for situational understanding and intelligent action, one is not primarily making predictions about what they will do in a given range of contexts. The complex and dynamic character of the unstructured situations which have to be handled requires that what constitutes an appropriate response has to be left open to the discretion of the practitioner (see also McClelland 1973). With respect to a teacher Pearson argues that 'we want to leave open the exact range of things they can do well, because teaching itself is such a broad activity that one cannot specify in advance all that the teacher will be called upon to do'. Pearson concludes that in attributing competence one is saying that, whatever an individual does in the circumstances they experience while performing an activity, they will do well.

Attributions of competence, on this alternative account of the concept of competence, do indeed give an assurance of quality but on a very different basis to attributions shaped by a behaviourist construct of competence. Rather than quality assurance resting on the capacity of a system to 'scientifically predict' the concrete performances of individuals, it rests on evidence of the general ability of individuals to act intelligently (wisely) in situations where a high degree of routinized behaviour is incommensurate with the realization of quality, e.g. in situations which involve communicative interaction. Implicit in this alternative construct of competence is a rather different conception of 'quality'. In this context 'quality' does not refer to a tangible end-product that conforms to prespecified functional standards. Rather it refers to the human values realized in social transactions between people. Thus the quality of a person's driving lies not so much in arriving at the intended destination, but in doing so having exercised due care and concern for the safety of others in the way the car was driven. Of course, such care and concern cannot be exercised without a great deal of technical skill, but it also depends on the driver's ability to grasp the evaluative significance of situations (s)he encounters and to make an appropriate response. This involves the exercise of powers to discern the meaning of events, to assess their practical significance and to decide on an appropriate response.

Within the context of a particular social practice, to act competently is to demonstrate abilities to realize the values – the obligations and responsibilities to others – which are intrinsic to good practice. The exercise of these abilities involves more than the use of habitual skill knowledge. What primarily demarcates the competent practitioners from the rest is their ability to exercise intelligent skill knowledge in fulfilling the responsibilities associated with their particular form of social practice.

Attributions of social competence do not predict future behaviour since what constitutes an appropriate realization of human value must be judged *in situ* rather than standardized and routinized. Therefore attempts to standardize what constitutes behavioural evidence of competence are misguided. The absence of standardized measures of behaviour does not, contrary to behaviourist dogma, imply the impossibility of making valid inferences from performance data, and publicly justifying them.

Looked at from this alternative point of view, competence in teaching rests on the powers of teachers to realize educational values in their transactions with students. The realization of these values establishes the conditions of a worthwhile process of teaching and learning. What is to count as a worthwhile process cannot be reduced to outcome measures of its instrumental effectiveness. The quality of learning outcomes are logically dependent upon the *educational quality* of the transactions between teachers and students, as Stenhouse (1971, 1975) so articulately argued in his seminal critique of the objectives model of curriculum design. One cannot reduce judgements about the educational quality of the transactions between teachers and students to measures of their instrumental effectiveness in producing prespecified and standardized outputs.

What is at stake here are two quite separate views of teaching; namely, of teaching as a technology versus teaching as a moral practice. Aoki (1984), for example, argues that 'teaching competence' takes on a very different meaning if one construes teaching as a practical (ethical) endeavour rather than as a form of instrumental action. The distinction goes back as far as Aristotle's *Ethics* and has been extensively employed by such curriculum theorists as Schwab (1970), Reid (1978), Carr and Kemmis (1986) and Elliott (1983, 1987, 1989a) to articulate a view of teaching as a form of practical inquiry/reflection which is quite distinct from the instrumental reasoning that characterizes technology. This view is now embodied in emerging new concepts of teacher professional development, such as 'teachers as action researchers' (Stenhouse 1975; Elliott 1985 and 1989b; Carr and Kemmis 1986; Whitehead 1989), and 'teachers as reflective practitioners' (Schon 1983, 1987; Russell 1988; Zeichner 1981, 1983).

Research informed by a non-behaviourist view of competence, which avoids the assumption that attributions of competence always function as predictions of behaviour, could make an important contribution to our understanding of what is involved in designing professional development programmes and forms of assessment which support reflective practice. The kinds of intelligent skill knowledge Pearson associates with situational understanding and intelligent practice appear to describe capacities teachers would need to develop as reflective practitioners and action researchers.

The recently defunct Training Agency, now replaced by regional Training Enterprise Councils (TECs), took the knowledge/competence issue on to its agenda, especially with respect to education and training in the professions. For example, it recently commissioned the Centre for Applied Research in Education at the University of East Anglia to undertake a fundamental study of the relationship between knowledge and competence across a range of professions.

Another, not unrelated, criticism of the behaviourist construct of job competence is that competence is not so much a characteristic of the job as a characteristic of those who perform the job well. On this view one cannot describe competence on the basis of job task/functions analysis. Instead one must describe what it is which people, judged to be competent, bring to the job. This view has formed the basis of an alternative methodology, for identifying and describing competence, pioneered by Harvard psychologist, D. C. McClelland (1973, 1976), and his associates at McBer and Company (Klemp 1977; Spencer 1979). They have argued that the acquisition of technical knowledge and skill does not characterize the difference between good performers and the minimally competent. Both may possess the requisite technical knowledge and skill, which although necessary, are not sufficient conditions of competent performances. This claim is consistent with McClelland's contention (see 1973) that competence cannot be operationally defined in terms of performance outcomes when it involves performing well in unstructured situations, where the appropriate response cannot be predicted in advance.

McBer and Company have significantly developed their methodology of job-competence assessment for public service and business professionals, the occupational domains where a strictly behaviourist construct of competence appears to encounter considerable resistance. The McBer methodology aims to identify and describe the abilities which differentiate practitioners judged by insiders to be 'above average' from those judged to be less competent but satisfying minimal standards. As yet it has had little impact on the work of the NCVQ and TA and is rarely cited in the growing UK literature on CBET and its assessment. It gets a single reference in the papers presented to the recent NCVQ conference on CBET in higher education at Sussex University. Tuxworth (1989) briefly described it as an alternative to task/functions analysis and claims it has 'had some influence' on management education in both the USA and UK.

McBer's job-competence assessment process moves through a series of steps:

1 **Identify the most effective performers of the job**

Immediate supervisor and peer rankings are frequently employed to select a group of 'above average' and a group of 'average' performers. Together they constitute a Criterion Sample. According to Spencer (1979) intuitive rankings by immediate supervisors and peers have a high degree of criterion validity but can be usefully supplemented by subordinate and client ratings.

Other approaches to identifying job-performance characteristics are regarded as more problematic by McBer Associates. The limitations attributed to job-tasks/functions analysis has already been considered. In addition characteristics identified by expert panels or derived from theoretical perspectives (e.g. humanistic psychology) are believed to lack supporting empirical data which shows how they are linked to job performance. According to Spencer both methods tend to generate moral virtues like 'integrity', 'perseverance' and 'courage'. But it is not easy to see how they relate to the quality of on-the-job performance. Successful performances may require the exercise of such virtues but they do not explain what distinguishes good performers from barely acceptable ones. One can perform with integrity, perseverance and courage and nevertheless perform rather badly. At best the characteristics derived from expert panels and theoretical models are a source of hypotheses whose significance must be empirically determined (see below, for example).

2 **Establish performance characteristics hypotheses**

An expert panel of experienced performers and observers of the job is 'convened to develop a list of hypothesized characteristics of people who do the job well.' Each characteristic is rated on four scales (see Spencer 1979):

- Whether it distinguishes superior from average.
- How many barely acceptable performers possess it.
- Its criticality for selection and training.
- How many job openings could realistically be filled if the characteristic was required as an entry criterion.

The more a characteristic is rated as distinguishing superior or above average performers, being possessed by few minimally acceptable ones, being critical for selection and training, and a realistic requirement, then the higher it is rated. Such an analysis provides a set of hypotheses about the critical characteristics of competence to be empirically verified through interview and observation.

3 **Behavioural-event interviews**

Superior and average performers are interviewed in depth about one or more 'critical situations' they have recently handled. Interviewees are asked to describe the situation in considerable narrative detail, and to reflect about the manner in which they handled it.

4 **Analysis of interview protocols to identify characteristics distinguishing superior from average performers**

Two or more trained analysts work on the data to infer *patterns* (rather than specific behaviours) which distinguish superior from average performers. Descriptions of patterns are refined until they become acceptable to all those involved in the analysis. They are then entered into a code book which outlines the competency model (structure) of the job.

The analysis tends to yield relatively few distinguishing patterns compared to the vast lists of behaviours produced by job-tasks/functions analyses. This is because 'patterns' consist of inferences from the data of underlying abilities which structure performance. Competence is viewed as a structure of abilities manifest in behaviour, rather than as atomistic elements of behaviour.

5 **Follow-up observations of selected individuals within each sample**

Feasible observational data is collected about the practice of selected individuals from each sample and analysed to determine the extent to which it confirms/disconfirms the inferences drawn from the behavioural-event interview data. As a result changes and refinements can be made to the initial descriptions of distinguishing characteristics.

6 **Cross-validation of competency model**

The competency model derived from an initial criterion sample is tested against a second criterion sample to see if it discriminates between 'good' and 'average' performers within the initial sample. Behavioural-event interview data is coded for the presence or absence of patterns which distinguished the two groups within the first criterion sample.

Sometimes behavioural-event interviews with a second criterion sample are replaced or supplemented by tests of operant behaviour, i.e. self-determined behaviour in unstructured situations, in contrast to behaviour governed by rules which specify correct responses. Operant tests simulate real job situations and provide individuals with opportunities to demonstrate an ability, identified as critical from the first criterion sample, without predetermining the behavioural outcome of any such demonstration. Spencer (1979), for example, contrasts an operant test for the ability to make an effective argument in a situation with a multiple choice test requiring respondents to recognize such an argument.

The criteria for scoring operant-test responses refer to conceptual elements of the critical ability to be demonstrated rather than to its behavioural manifestations. The extent to which the test response meets the criteria for the ability in question is a matter of interpretation rather than straightforward observation.

Spencer (1979) provides an example of a system for scoring the extent to which performance in operant-test situations manifests the critical ability called 'accurate empathy'. The concept is defined in terms of the ability to grasp accurately the *content, meaning* and *feeling* of what a person says. These three conceptual aspects of empathy provide the criteria for assessing the extent to which it is manifested in performance. If the response indicates a failure to grasp what someone is talking about, why they are doing so and how they feel about the situation, then it is given the lowest score – 1 – on a four-point scale. If the content only is accurately grasped, then the response gets a 2 rating. If content and meaning are both grasped but not how the other feels, then the response gets a rating of 3. When all three aspects are grasped a 4 rating is merited.

It should be emphasized that assessment levels of this kind refer to the extent to which an ability is manifested in behaviour and not to stages in its development. I shall discuss the problem of identifying developmental stages later.

Operant-test responses, scored against conceptual criteria in the way described, can validate a competency model generated from a first criterion sample if they differentiate individuals designated 'above average' or 'good', from those designated 'average'. In doing so they justify some confidence in the predictive validity of the competence model. However, prediction in this context refers to a potential to do a job well rather than to a specific set of behaviours. The competency models derived from McBer's job-competency assessment method constitute a rather different form of quality assurance to those derived from job-tasks/functions analysis methods.

Professional competence and the development of situational understanding

The competency models developed by McBer for a variety of organizations, are highly consistent with Pearson's view that competence largely consists of abilities involved in developing insight into practical situations, and how to respond intelligently in them: what he calls 'intelligent skill knowledge'.

In a summary of a variety of job-competence analyses carried out by McBer and Company from 1972–7, Klemp (1977) identified a number of critical abilities which generalized across a diversity of occupations that involve problem-solving and decision-making in complex situations. In doing so, he avoided assuming transfer of skills exercised in one occupational context to another. For example, the fact that empathy is a critical ability in a number of occupations does not necessarily imply that someone who is able to empathize with people encountered in one job context will be able to do so with those (s)he would encounter in another job context. The organizational culture in the latter context, for example, may be antithetical to human relations based on empathy. However, given some similarities in the organizational cultures which shape social interaction, and in the categories of people encountered, one can reasonably expect a degree of 'transfer of skills' from one job context to another.

First of all, Klemp, in describing a general model of occupational competence, identifies a group of closely related *cognitive abilities* which are commonly exercised by above-average performers. He distinguishes these from information-processing skills which are related to abilities to memorize and recall propositional theoretical knowledge, describing the cognitive abilities as 'conceptual skills which bring order to the informational chaos that constantly surrounds us.' Inasmuch as they underpin the acquisition and use of knowledge, the knowledge referred to is situational knowledge based on the experience of particular aspects of the situations encountered. The abilities exercised and developed in the acquisition of situational knowledge 'transcend analysis . . . and are closer in spirit to the ability to synthesize information from a prior analysis through a process of induction.'

Klemp identifies three cognitive abilities which are critical for situational understanding in a number of occupational settings. They are:

• *Discerning thematic consistencies* in diverse information and organizing and communicating them.

- *Understanding controversial issues* at stake in conflicts between people, and the different perspectives the conflicting parties hold.
- *Learning from reflection on experience* by observing and analysing one's own behaviour in the context of the behaviour of others in a situation.

Secondly, Klemp identifies a group of *interpersonal abilities* as common characteristics of good performers. They are:

- *Accurate empathy*, which 'give[s] clients and co-workers the message that not only is something being said or done in a way that they can understand, but also that the clients and co-workers are themselves understood.'
- *Promoting feelings of efficacy in others*. This ability is closely linked to empathy in the sense that the latter is a necessary condition of exercising it. Promoting feelings of efficacy has, according to Klemp, three aspects: positive regard for others, giving others active support and controlling impulsive feelings of hostility or anger which, if released, would make another person feel powerless and ineffective.

A third cluster of abilities is related to and depends upon certain kinds of *motivation*. One kind is *achievement motivation*: the need to do something better than it has been done before by oneself or others. The abilities which primarily satisfy this need are:

- *Risk-taking*: To take moderate risks in certain situations, to achieve something new and original.
- *Goal setting*: To set time-phased, realistic goals.
- *Eliciting feedback*: To seek information for use as feedback on one's own performance.

Another kind of motivation is a form of *power motivation*: the need to exert influence in the service of organizational goals. The abilities involved in satisfying this need are:

- *Networking*: the ability to learn interpersonal influence networks and use them to do the job.
- *Goal-sharing*: the ability to influence others by sharing with them a super-ordinate goal.
- *Micropolitical awareness*: the ability to identify work-group coalitions with regard to both their level in the hierarchy and their orientation to the goals of the organization.

Klemp claims that underpinning achievement and power motivation and their associated abilities is a fundamental ability called *cognitive initiative* which refers to the way performers define themselves as actors in a situation. It is related to whether they see themselves as capable of changing a situation rather than as helpless victims of events.

The three clusters of abilities cited by Klemp exemplify what I have called 'a structure of competence'. Abilities are not isolated discrete elements but are linked together structurally. For example, each of the three clusters is unified by an overarching category which is presupposed by the other characteristics. The unifying categories of ability are *synthesizing parts into wholes, empathy*, and *cognitive initiative*. They can also be linked together as *powers of practical understanding*, i.e. capacities for developing insights into complex, fluid, human situations which enable participants in them to act wisely. Practical understanding is 'insider knowledge' and grounded in an awarenes of the self as an active agent in the situations one experiences, and therefore as one who is capable of influencing the lives of others. This awareness (cognitive initiative) generates ethical obligations with respect to the care and concern for others one exercises in the pursuit of goals. In order to exercise such care and concern one needs to be able to understand the thoughts and feelings of others in the situation (empathy). Empathy is necessary to building a total picture of the situation (synthesizing parts into wholes) which enables one to act wisely in it.

This account of the structural principles embedded in Klemp's general model of occupational competence supports the view expressed earlier that competence has an ethical dimension, involving the realization of ethical obligations in the way the goals of an activity are pursued. Competence exercised in the context of complex social practices is never pure instrumental effectiveness. The structural principles also illuminate the relationship between knowledge and competence. The critical abilities exercised by competent practitioners are underpinned by mental powers exercised in developing situational knowledge. This knowledge cannot be reduced to information and rules expressed in propositional form. It is knowledge based on direct experience which gets stored in memory, not as sets of propositions but as a repertoire of case narratives. Hence the methodological significance of McBer's emphasis on behavioural–event interview data in job-competence assessment.

There is little evidence that the McBer approach to identifying critical abilities has been widely used by public education and training agencies in the UK. The author (see Elliott 1988a) undertook a small-scale investigation of abilities evidenced in the practices of police patrol officers. Behavioural-event interviews were conducted with a criterion sample of 24 officers (12 designated 'above average' and 12 as 'average'). The sample consisted of three sub-samples drawn from different policing environments: rural, inner urban, and 'new town'. Most of the abilities inferred from the interview data could be clustered under four broad categories:

- synthesizing information and observational data into a total picture of the situation.
- awareness of other people's feelings and concerns (empathy).

- exercising initiative and taking decisive action (proactivity).
- reflecting upon one's actions and their consequences in the situation.

Although there was a tendency for abilities linked to empathy and proactivity to be more frequently evidenced in the data drawn from the above-average group, it was abilities related to synthesizing parts into 'total pictures of the situation' and to self-reflection which were most evidenced in the interview data from the above average group.

The police study was carried out as part of a collaborative effort, supported by the Home Office, between the police service and academics based in the Centre for Applied Research in Education at the University of East Anglia. The project was to develop a new national curriculum and assessment system for police probationer training. The findings of the study were incorporated into a competency model which informed the design of the curriculum and a system for profiling the professional development of police probationers.

The development of competence

One possible criticism of the McBer methodology is the rather crude way it classifies individuals into 'above average' and 'average' categories. In defence it could be argued that these are the common-sense categories expressed in the intuitive comparisons of 'insiders' and must form the basis of any method which attempts to describe what is being intuitively distinguished in these comparisons of performers. However, one can accept the claim of McBer's associates that these common-sense categories discriminate levels of ability, but still ask whether it is possible to improve on the categories 'insiders' employ in assessments of personnel. The common-sense categories employed in McBer's job-competence assessment method may be a sufficient basis on which to yield information that can help managers make better decisions about the selection and deployment of staff. However, these categories may be rather more limited as a basis for generating information which is useful to staff developers.

McClelland and his associates claim that the abilities their method discriminates can be developed through training and have designed a process for doing so. In my view the process would be enhanced if it were informed by an empirically grounded model which discriminated levels of development in the acquisition of abilities which characterize good performers. Fortunately Dreyfus (1981) has provided an empirically grounded account of the development of the kinds of abilities the McBer methodology is concerned with. It is also consistent with Pearson's view of competence as the exercise of 'intelligent skill knowledge'.

According to Dreyfus the acquisition of skill in relation to complex human activities, such as business management, is largely a matter of learning to understand and judge situations. He identifies four mental capacities involved: *component recognition, salience recognition, whole-situation recognition* and *decision-making*. The components of a situation are either objective context-free attributes or subjectively experienced context-dependent aspects.

The raw novice can be taught to recognize objective attributes 'without benefit of experience'. Thus, 'The student driver is taught to recognize such interpretation-free features as instrument readings and separation distances, and is given rules for when it is safe to enter traffic and at what speed to shift gears.' Dreyfus calls this kind of component recognition *non-situational*. The ability to recognize context-dependent aspects depends on prior experience of real situations in which 'the performer notes, or a mentor points out, recurrent meaningful situational components.' Examples provided by Dreyfus, from chess-playing and business respectively, are 'weak pawn-structure on the King's side' and 'poor product positioning'.

Salience recognition involves discriminating which attributes and aspects of a situation need to be considered in forming a judgement about how to respond in it. Whole-situation recognition can be either analytically or holistic-ally derived. When it is analytically derived a person will consciously consider all the salient attributes and aspects of a situation and deduce a total picture of his/her circumstances from them. When a grasp of the total situation is holistic, all the salient components will be intuitively synthesized into a total picture without prior reflection. Decisions which are made in the light of situational understanding may be rational or intuitive. Rational decisions flow from a process of conscious reasoning about how, given a certain understanding of the situation, one ought to respond in it. Intuitive decisions involve no such reasoning. Intuitive decisions accompany whole-situation recognition without much prior reflection and planning.

Having identified different forms in which capacities for situational under-standing and judgement are manifested, Dreyfus produces a five-stage model of their combined development (see Table 8.1).

It is illuminating to consider the models of occupational competence

Table 8.1 Five-stage model of development of situational understanding and judgement (Dreyfus 1981)

	Component recognition	Salience recognition	Whole-situation recognition	Decision
1 Novice	non-situational	none	analytical	rational
2 Advanced beginner	situational	none	analytical	rational
3 Competent	situational	present	analytical	rational
4 Proficient	situational	present	holistic	rational
5 Expert	situational	present	holistic	intuitive

generated by the McBer method in the light of this developmental scheme. Dreyfus argues that advanced beginners represent a marginally acceptable level of performance. They are able to interpret meaningful aspects of situations, unlike novices. But they are not yet able to discriminate between aspects in terms of their implications for decision-making. Decisions are governed by principles or guidelines: fail-safe devices which cover all eventualities by treating 'all attributes and aspects as equally important and are formulated so as to integrate as many as possible.' The competence models which the McBer method produces emphasize conceptual abilities which appear to be related to discriminating salient attributes and aspects of situations. Similarly, it can be argued that the kinds of abilities identified as distinguishing characteristics in the areas of interpersonal relations and achievement and power motivation, express or presuppose a capacity for discriminating which attributes and aspects are important to consider when making decisions.

In the Dreyfus model the emergence of the kinds of abilities identified by the McBer method are a feature of the competence stage. The conceptual abilities are essential for reflecting analytically about one's experience of situations, but they are largely transcended at the later stages of proficiency and expertise by the ability to recognize holistically the meaning and significance of all the relevant aspects of situations. We can therefore draw the conclusion that the common-sense categories of 'average' and 'below average' employed by McBer are essentially differentiating people still largely operating at the advanced-beginner stage (even if no longer beginners in a literal sense) from those who have achieved a large measure of competence.

The McBer studies appear to sample performers operating at stages 2 and 3. One might expect this in a context where the major concern of management is with the selection and promotion of early to mid-career personnel who have more job experience than novices but less than that required for proficiency and expertise. As Dreyfus points out, the development of capacities for situational understanding depends upon the accumulation of experience. The proficient and the expert will tend to have moved beyond that career phase in which their skill development depends on the outcome of formal job selection procedures and the provision of formal training.

The Dreyfus model illuminates rather than undermines the McBer methodology. But in doing so it reveals its limitations as a basis for describing the ways in which structures of human abilities change and develop with increasing amounts of hands-on experience. For example, looked at in the light of the stage model we can explain why theoretical knowledge is not a characteristic which distinguishes 'above average' from 'average performers'. It plays a major role in analytic situational understanding at the novice and advanced-beginner stages, but a more subsidiary role at the competence stage where analytic situational analysis subordinates it to reflection, grounded in experience, about the practical significance of attributes and aspects of the situation. At stages 4 and 5 theoretical modelling of situational components is completely transcended and replaced by holistic knowledge encapsulated in repertoires of cases stored in memory.

The Dreyfus model also illuminates the relationship between the general model of professional competence produced by the McBer method and ideas like 'reflective practice' and 'action research' which articulate a contemporary approach to professional learning and development. Like the general findings of the McBer studies, such ideas can be located at the competence stage in the Dreyfus model, where practice is grounded in a form of analytical situational understanding which requires practitioners to exercise their capacities for reflection. We may therefore claim that action research is the process by which the structure of abilities that define competent professional practice are most fully realized in those practitioners who aspire to develop their skills a stage beyond that of the advanced beginner.

Concluding remarks

We have the conceptual tools and the basis of a research methodology to enable us to generate competency models which are credible to both professionals (including teachers) and policy makers, because they will be both developmentally orientated and provide a basis for a system of quality assurance (accountability). The latter will aim to predict and control the quality of professional practice without predicting and controlling the specific actions and responses of practitioners.

With respect to the teaching profession we need a programme of research capable of generating a non-behaviourist model of the development of those ability structures which are both central to teachers' professional powers of self-determination and provide policy makers with an assurance of quality. Such a model would give the teaching profession, or their educators in higher-education institutions, less reason to fear competency-based assessment, training and selection. With respect to teacher education and training the model might well throw new light on the significance of theoretical knowledge for the practices of novice teachers and advanced beginners, as well as on the significance of reflective practice for the development of teaching competence. The model could well legitimate the involvement of higher-education institutions in an appraisal process which profiles the continuous development of teachers' abilities.

9

The National Curriculum and models of curriculum development

This final chapter looks at the planning model which underpins the National Curriculum and Stenhouse's critique of that model. It describes Stenhouse's alternative 'process model' and locates it in a tradition of thought which stems from Aristotle.

The author indicates how a national curriculum shaped by a process model would differ from the one enshrined in the Education Reform Act. He concludes by clarifying the role of reflective practitioners in a process-oriented national curriculum.

The legacy of Lawrence Stenhouse

Lawrence Stenhouse spent a great deal of his professional life attacking the intrusion of 'technical rationality' into curriculum planning. In the late 1960s this view of practical reasoning appeared in the guise of 'rational curriculum planning'. Curriculum planning, it was argued (see Kerr 1968), could only be rational if it were guided by quite clear and specific statements of intended learning outcomes, defined in terms of measurable changes in student behaviour. Rational planning proceeds by breaking down general aims into more tangible objectives and then selecting learning experiences to achieve them. The assumptions about rationality which underpinned this planning model were as follows:

- Questions about the ends of human activities can be separated from questions about how to realize them.
- The value of human activities resides in their instrumental (or technical)

effectiveness in bringing about desirable outcomes which are extrinsic to
the activities themselves. Extrinsic outcomes alone justify the means.

● Human activities can be justified only if their outcomes refer to observable
changes.

● Rational action proceeds from a prior process of instrumental (technical)
reasoning about how to achieve tangible results.

Stenhouse (1975) claimed that 'the objectives model' of curriculum planning
was anti-educational and proposed an alternative: 'the process model'. He
drew inspiration from the work of R. S. Peters who by the 60s had turned his
considerable talents and energies to the task of elucidating the nature of
education. According to Peters (1959), our everyday discourse about the aims
of education does not assume that we are talking about the extrinsic outcomes
of a process. Rather, Peters argued, we are referring to values and principles
which constitute a process as an *educational* one. 'Aims' in educational
discourse referred to procedural criteria or principles which were realized *in*
rather than as a result of the process of education. Stenhouse developed his
process model' on this 'insight'. In Chapters 1 and 2 I argued that such an
insight was actually embodied in the curriculum-reform practices of many
teachers in secondary modern schools during the 60s. What Peters and
Stenhouse did was to articulate a logic, an alternative form of practical
rationality, that was already implicit in the practices of innovatory teachers. I
shall explore the implications of this point for curriculum planning at the end
of the paper.

Stenhouse's great contribution was to design the Humanities Curriculum
Project (see Stenhouse 1968) as an illustration of the radical contrast between
the 'process' and 'objectives' models. He began, not with the question 'what are
the objectives of the curriculum?' but with a problem situation that faced
teachers attempting to make the secondary-school curriculum of the 60s more
relevant to the lives of young adolescents. The problem was 'how do teachers
handle value issues in classrooms within a pluralistic democracy'?

He ruled out two answers to the problem (see Stenhouse 1971). First, he
argued that, if education was to be a preparation for life, value issues should be
part of the explicit content of the curriculum. This view in itself sanctioned
innovation since the curriculum in all schools largely reflected the academic
curriculum of the grammar schools. It was largely subject based and exclusively concerned with the transmission of factual information. The values
implicit in the selection of facts and the human purposes they served were not
generally brought to the surface and discussed. Second, Stenhouse ruled out
the possibility that teachers should use their authority position to promote
their own personal commitments. He argued that this was inconsistent with the
democratic rights of parents and communities not to have the values they
subscribed to undermined by teachers who were committed to different value
positions.

So Stenhouse ruled out two responses to the problem. In doing so he ruled out two kinds of aims: the acquisition of knowledge detached from consideration of questions of value, and the inculcation of a particular value position. This allowed a third alternative solution to emerge: namely, that students should develop their understanding of human actions and situations in the light of the controversial value issues they raised. This aim specifies a learning process rather than an extrinsic outcome of learning. Stenhouse refused to specify what the outcome of the process would consist of but argued that it implied a set of procedural principles. First, that controversial issues should form part of the content of the curriculum in schools. Second, that discussion of issues rather than didactic instruction should constitute the core of the classroom process. Third, that teachers should refrain from using classrooms as a platform for promoting their views. Fourth, that divergence in discussion should be protected. Fifth, that teachers had responsibility for the critical standards employed in the discussion, e.g. ensuring that views and arguments were tested against standards of reasoning and evidence.

The Humanities Project was designed as a specification of a worthwhile 'educational' process of teaching and learning about value issues, without determining precisely what the outcomes would be. It was presumed that these would constitute divergent interpretations of controversial human acts and situations, grounded in different value positions. What such a process does is provide students with opportunities to modify and reconstruct their values in the light of alternative perspectives.

Underpinning the 'process model' is a totally different logic of reasoning to that of technical rationality:

- Questions about ends cannot be separated from questions about means.
- The value of human activities lies in their intrinsic qualities. Ends justify means because they specify qualities realized in the activities (processes) themselves. They are not extrinsically related outcomes.
- Activities are justified by their intrinsic ends, and these do not refer to observable effects. They are justified, not on the basis of observable effects, but on the basis of judgemental inferences about the manner in which they are performed.
- Rational action proceeds from practical deliberation about how to realize ends-in-view *in* concrete activities within particular complex situations. Such ends-in-view cannot be operationally defined in terms of the means they are constituted by in advance of the situation. Means are determined *in situ* and therefore always involved an element of 'shooting in the dark'. There is a sense in which the ends are operationally defined through the selection of the means to realize them. In abstract form they remain essentially vague. If asked for operational definitions, one can only cite concrete instances of their realization in particular circumstances. Ends are therefore only clarified by reflection on the experience of particular

attempts to realize them in action. In selecting means, people also operationally define their ends-in-view. Practical deliberation involves reflecting
about means and ends together.

In his *Ethics* Aristotle argued for a distinction between activities which
constitute the *making* of a product and those which involved *doing* something
well (see Elliott 1983). Technical rationality, or *techne* as he called it, is the form
of reasoning appropriate to the making of products, while practical deliberation, or *phronesis*, is the form of reasoning appropriate to doing something
well. These two forms of rationality, underpinning the 'objectives' and 'process' models of curriculum planning, have been around a long time. What
Stenhouse objected to was the encroachment of technical rationality into our
thinking about education, and its transformation from a practice in the
Aristotelian sense of the term to a technology.

Stenhouse died in 1982. What would he make of the 1988 Educational
Reform Act (ERA) as it casts its shadow across the educational land-
scape? Professor Brian Simon, in his passionate critique of Kenneth Baker's
'reforms' at a British Educational Research Association conference, suggested that Stenhouse was surely 'turning in his grave' over a bill that so
clearly undermined his life's work. I cannot predict his response. Of
one thing I am sure; it would be an unusually creative and unpredictable
one.

All we can do is to draw on the legacy of Stenhouse's ideas in formulating our
response to the National Curriculm. This is not simply a matter of applying his
ideas to the ERA. These ideas were essentially developed as a critical response
to the problems and issues posed by the curriculum-reform movement of the
late 60s and 70s. What is required now is a critical response to the problems
and issues of the late 80s and 90s. Stenhouse's legacy was to draw on a
tradition of thinking about social practices, such as education, which goes back
as far as Aristotle. This tradition is increasingly being drawn on by philosophers
and social theorists who feel that the encroachment of technical rationality into
every area of social life is endangering fundamental human values. In trying to
discern what is at stake in our response to the ERA, we may need to draw even
more extensively on the Aristotelian tradition than Stenhouse did. This does
not mean that we have to read Aristotle. Stenhouse, to my knowledge, never
cited him. Nor did he cite Gadamer (1975) who reconstructed Aristotle's
thought as a basis for a critique of technical rationality. One can secure access to
a tradition as a resource for one's thinking, without being able to locate the
source of the ideas it embodies. Traditions of thought are embedded in our
culture. Moreover, they are dynamic, evolving historically as they are applied to
new problems and issues which emerge in society. Traditions which ossify and
fail to accommodate social change die. Traditions of thought not only evolve
and change but they contain features which endure over time. It is the basic
unchanging structure of ideas that underpins a tradition of thought which we

need to grasp in working out the implications of that tradition for our response to a particular historically situated social situation.

Education as a social practice

Perhaps the most trenchant analysis of the condition of contemporary Western society to be published in recent years was provided by Alasdair MacIntyre in *After Virtue* (1981). In his book MacIntyre argues that the condition is grave and can be redeemed only if we protect and preserve forms of social life which conform to the Aristotelian ethical tradition. In Chapter 14 MacIntyre sketches what he believes to be the core features of that tradition which I shall now attempt to summarize.

Central to the Aristotelian ethical tradition is the exercise of the virtues. The idea of virtue derives its sense from and can only be sustained in social practices. According to MacIntyre a social practice is:

> any coherent and complex form of socially established co-operative human activity through which goods internal to that form of activity are realized in the course of trying to achieve those standards of excellence which are appropriate to, and partially definitive of that form of activity, with the result that human powers to achieve excellence, and human conceptions of the ends and goods involved, are systematically extended.

MacIntyre argues that, on this account of a social practice, only some activities are complex enough to count as social practices. What are ruled out are activities which require a limited range of technical skills, e.g. throwing a football, bricklaying, planting turnips. However, these simple activities form part of more complex activities: playing football, architecture, farming. It is the latter which constitute social practices.

Social practices cannot be understood as aggregations of simple technical skill domains. Achieving excellence in a social practice is not just a matter of improving specific technical skills. It also involves having regard for the ends and values which define the practice and developing those powers which are necessary if they are to be realized.

The distinction between goods (values) internal to a practice and goods external to it is a crucial one. External goods are only contingently connected to a practice. If one cannot obtain such things as prestige, status or wealth as a result of participation in a certain practice, there are always alternative means available of obtaining them. However, goods internal to a practice can be obtained only by engaging in that particular practice. They consist of complex abilities and skills which can be developed only in the pursuit of goals which are intrinsic to the practice and give it its point. This pursuit of intrinsic goals is governed by standards and principles of procedure against which perform- ance in the activity is judged. MacIntyre claims that over time conceptions of the goals intrinsic to a practice change and with them the standards and principles which govern their pursuit. These in turn call forth new extensions of human powers and therefore new conceptions of the internal goods which can be achieved. By way of illustration MacIntyre shows how the goals of portrait painting have shifted from the iconic representations of Christ and the saints, through the naturalist representations of actual faces in 15th-century Flemish and German painting, to the synthesis of Rembrandt where the naturalistic portrait of a particular individual is rendered in a novel iconic form.

It is in relation to Aristotelian accounts of a social practice that MacIntyre defines a virtue as:

> an acquired human quality the possession and exercise of which tends to enable us to achieve those goods which are internal to practices and lack of which effectively prevents us from achieving any such goods.

In addition to virtues specific to a particular social practice, MacIntyre suggests there are certain virtues which are necessary to sustain social practices in general, e.g. those of justice, courage and honesty. He also argues that any adequate concept of these more general virtues assumes some holistic view of the goals and goods of human life generally. Without such a view human life lacks unity and is pervaded with conflicts between incompatible social practices, e.g. between commitments to excellence in the arts and the claims of family life. One needs, he argues, some over-arching view of the purpose of life to be able to prioritize and organize our commitment to specific social practices.

MacIntyre uses his Aristotelian account of a social practice to throw light on the issue of competition versus co-operation in human activities. There is an important difference between external and internal goods. When the former are achieved, they belong only to the individuals who achieve them. Those who fail to achieve them do not possess them. The achievement of external goods, given that not all can succeed, necessarily involves competition between individuals. However, those who achieve internal goods benefit the community of practitioners as a whole.

MacIntyre argues that when Turner 'transformed the seascape in painting' in a quite new way he 'enriched the whole relevant community.' Of course, MacIntyre points out, people do compete to excel in a social practice but their shared commitment to its goals enables them to appreciate and rejoice in the excellence achieved by others. While external goods benefit only individuals, internal goods benefit communities. They are common rather than individual goods. But even the excellence achieved by individuals within a social practice is the outcome of social co-operation operating through the exercise of virtues such as treating others justly, being honest or truthful (not cheating), and putting oneself at risk to protect others from harm (moral courage). MacIntyre argues that:

without the virtues there could be a recognition only of what I have called external goods and not at all of internal goods in the context of practices. And in any society which recognized only external goods competitiveness would be the dominant and even exclusive feature.

Finally, MacIntyre is careful to distinguish a social practice from its institutional context. Institutions are necessary to sustain social practices. Medicine needs hospitals, education needs schools and intellectual disciplines need universities. It is through an institution that people are initiated into a social practice, thereby learning to acquire its virtues and submitting themselves to its standards. However, institutions as such are inevitably concerned with the acquisition and distribution of external goods such as wealth, power and status. And indeed, MacIntyre argues, such concerns are necessary if institutions are to support and sustain social practices. The relationship between external and internal goods is an intimate one. But it does make social practices particularly vulnerable to the competitiveness of institutions. This is why the virtues are so important. 'Without justice, courage, and honesty', MacIntyre argues, 'practices could not resist the corrupting power of institutions.' In other words, the achievement of the virtues gives participants in a social practice the power not only to achieve excellence in their performance but to resist the corrupting influence of naked competition for wealth, status and power.

Stenhouse on 'education'

It is interesting to compare MacIntyre's reiteration of the Aristotelian tradition with Stenhouse's (1975) discussion of the way in which the universal application of 'the objectives model' to curriculum planning would distort the nature of education. Stenhouse argued that education is necessarily comprised of four processes: training, instruction, initiation and induction. Training is concerned with the acquisition of skills involved in the performance of a specific task, e.g. making a canoe, learning a foreign language, typing, baking a cake, handling laboratory apparatus. His examples resemble Aristotle's *making* activities, and those proffered by MacIntyre as technical skill domains. Instruction is concerned with the acquisition and retention of information, e.g. tables of chemical elements, dates in history, the names of European countries, German irregular verbs, a pastry recipe. According to Stenhouse 'the objectives model' is appropriate to designing training and instructional processes. But although a necessary part of educational activity, these processes are not sufficient to make it educational.

Initiation is concerned with securing commitment and conformity to certain social norms and values. These are frequently not made explicit but are tacitly transmitted through the 'hidden curriculum'. Induction is concerned with giving access to knowledge. But knowledge is not the same as information.

Rather, according to Stenhouse, it constitutes structures or systems of thinking, about ourselves and the world, which are encapsulated within our culture. For Stenhouse induction into systems of thought is central to any *educational* process. As features of such a process, training, instruction and initiation are all subordinate processes. Moreover, Stenhouse argues, induction cannot be matched to 'the objectives model'. This is because knowledge is not information but structures 'to sustain creative thought and provide frameworks for judgement.' However, such structures are intrinsically problematic and contestable in the sense that the theories, concepts and principles of which they consist are open to a variety of interpretations. Stenhouse argued, for example, that disputes amongst historians about the causes of war are not so much based on the evidence available to each party as on conflicting interpretations of the concept of historical causality. To translate 'structures' into 'objectives' or 'targets' is to distort the nature of knowledge.

Educationally speaking, it is not sufficient to transmit inert information about ideas, concepts and theories to students in the form of definitions. In the process of induction the teacher represents them as critical standards (s)he brings to bear on students' thinking about problems in the subject-matter. They are embedded in the questions (s)he poses, the evidence (s)he draws attention to, and the tests (s)he asks students to submit their thinking to. Moreover, the teacher should induct students in a manner which gives them access to the problematic and contestable nature of structures of knowledge. An educationally worthwhile process involves a reflexive attitude towards the nature of knowledge on the part of both teacher and students. Dialogue between teacher and students and discussion amongst students are procedural principles governing any educationally worthwhile induction into knowledge.

The process of induction is more concerned with the manner in which students think than with the precise outcome of that thinking. Inducting students into the structures of knowledge is not a matter of producing a standardized outcome, but of enabling them to think in the light of standards which define disciplined ways of thinking. The production of a uniformity of outcomes is an indication that students are not developing their own powers of understanding but merely reproducing the understandings of their teachers. Stenhouse writes:

> Consider the marking of history essays. The examination marker has a large number which he must monitor.
>
> As he reads them he often becomes aware that there is a depressing similarity about them. This is because the majority of teachers have been working to a behavioural objective . . . From the pile of essays a few leap out at the marker as original, surprising, showing evidence of individual thinking. These, the unpredictable, are the successes.

He argues that: 'Education as induction in knowledge is successful to the extent that it makes the behavioural outcomes of the students unpredictable.'

This account of the process of education makes it sound very much like a social practice. Knowledge as the end-in-view is not a product of an educational process which can be defined independently of it. It is the forms or systems of thought which shape the interaction between teachers and students and amongst students within an educational process. It refers to those standards of excellence which are brought to bear on students' thinking in a manner which activates and extends their natural powers of the understanding. It is the development of these powers which constitutes the goods internal to education and the achievement of excellence within it. Ray Elliott (1973) has argued that the natural powers of the human understanding are exercised:

> in retention and anticipation: synthesis and synopsis: in the reduction of wholes to parts: in bracketing properties and aspects: in discovering the objects of feelings and impressions: in guesswork: in pushing ideas to their limits: in shifts of perspective of many kinds: in weighing pros and cons and sensing the balance: and so on.

Knowledge constitutes the structures which have historically evolved in our society for performing these mental activities. Such structures are a medium in which to think and develop the powers of the understanding: powers which constitute internal qualities, rather than external products, of the mental activities Elliott cites.

One can think of the virtues which are necessary if people are to develop their powers of understanding within the educational process, e.g. those of curiosity, patience, tenacity, persistence, open-mindedness, intellectual courage, honesty with oneself and humility.

According to Stenhouse it is only when we have clarified knowledge as a medium rather than a product of thinking that we are in a position to grasp the functions of norms, information and skills within the educational process. We cannot break knowledge down into specific informational, skill and normative components and then treat them as objectives of an educational process. This kind of outlook will be familiar to all those teachers who have been advised to classify their curriculum aims as either 'concepts', 'skills' or 'attitudes'. To do this is to lose sight of the educative context in which information, skills and attitudes need to be transmitted. For Stenhouse education involves these other processes of transmission but it cannot be reduced to them without loss. They must always be subordinated to the overall aim of inducting students into structures of knowledge. In this context 'the objectives model' can be applied to designing instruction and training but it always plays a subordinate role to 'the process model'.

Excellence, standards and the ERA

In this section I shall critique, in the light of the previous sections, the assumptions about excellence and standards embodied in the ERA. As a springboard I want to describe an episode which occurred during a delegation to the Secretary of State from the 1988 North of England conference. In what appeared an unguarded moment Mr Baker, then Secretary of State for Education, confessed a concern that his proposed Act would do little to cater for creative learning. He experienced a tension between a curriculum which raised standards generally and one which catered for creativity. We all agreed that his curriculum left little space for creativity in learning but did not have time on a crowded agenda to explore the issue further. So let me try now.

The Minister in all his talk about 'raising standards' and achieving 'excellence' in education, misunderstood the nature of educational standards and confused them with product specifications or 'standardization'. This is because he had become trapped in a view of education as a manufacturing process or technology. In this context standards are concerned with securing a uniformity of product and defining fixed objectives or 'targets' as the government calls them: a military metaphor employed by business and industry as an orientation for the rational management of resources.

ERA assumed that in setting targets, the task groups would be establishing *educational* standards. Contrast this with Stenhouse's view that the quality of educational achievements is manifested in unpredictable and diverse performances. Induction into structures of knowledge does not standardize students' thinking but supports creativity and originality of thought. The Minister's 'dilemma' was experienced as such because he assumed that 'standards' define ends external to educational processes. If he viewed them as structures of thought which support the development of those natural powers which constitute goods internal to education and which manifest themselves in unpredictable and diverse performances, then he would experience no dilemma between 'raising standards' and an education for creativity.

The logic of 'technical rationality' pervades the ERA. Once educational standards are specified as measurable targets, which can be defined independently of the content and process of education, teachers have little option but to distort the practice of education and the role standards play in it. Stenhouse (1975, ch. 7) neatly illustrates the consequences of target setting when he argues that 'Literary skills are to be justified as helping us to read Hamlet. Hamlet must not be justified as a training ground for literary skills.' It is difficult to see how, under the provisions of the Act, teachers will be able to justify the content of education other than in terms of its instrumentality for achieving extrinsically related targets. A good example of the gradual capitulation of the task groups to the ruthless logic of 'technical rationality' can be found in the saga of the maths group. The original task group broke up in disarray after the majority refused to specify specific attainment targets for ages 7, 11, 14 and 16 and reaffirmed the emphasis in modern maths on the development of understanding. Professor Sig Prais resigned. He evidently believed that an emphasis on computational skills was the only way we could match the performance of German, French and Japanese students. He is a member of the National

Institute of Economic and Social Research which spends a great deal of time undertaking cross-national comparative studies of achievement.

The task group reconvened and produced attainment targets. However, according to the *Observer* (14 August 1988) the report reflected a continuing tendency to make computational skills subordinate to 'understanding'. Although structures of knowledge are represented as targets according to the rhetoric of government, they can easily be reinterpreted by teachers as criteria governing the process of learning. What is at stake here is the very idea of mathematics teaching as an educational practice and the achievement of excellence in relation to those goods which are internal to the process of developing mathematical understanding.

At another level one can argue that this saga of political manipulation has little to do with *educational* standards and excellence as such. First, it is about designing a competitive system of schooling: one which enables achievements to be compared with other advanced industrial countries. The only way this can be done is to specify achievements as quantifiable outcomes. And one can do this only if they are posited as goods which are extrinsic to the educational process; as information and skills which render those individuals who possess them saleable commodities on the labour market. The theory is that, if we gear schooling towards the acquisition of marketable facts and skills, our school system will not only compete successfully with other industrial societies, but this success will enable us to achieve supremacy in the industrial enterprise of wealth creation.

Within an enterprise which is exclusively concerned with transforming human beings into marketable commodities, there is little room for pupils to achieve those goods which are internal to educational practices; goods which can only be described as excellences of 'being'. The problem with the ERA is that it divorces 'standards' from 'human excellence'. And this is why there is no room for creativity. An educational system which exclusively aims to transform people into commodities for consumption on the labour market must treat them in turn as passive consumers. The curriculum will consist of objects to be possessed in the form of facts and skills rather than objects of thought: situations, problems and issues which are capable of challenging, activating and extending natural powers of being. Only a curriculum of the latter kind can provide a context for the achievement of human excellence.

To borrow Erich Fromm's (1976) distinction between the 'being' and 'having' modes of human existence I would argue that the ERA as politically conceived, constitutes a comprehensive plan for generating an 'education for having' and eliminating any 'subversive' attempts to establish an 'education for being'. Such a conception reinforces a view of pupils and their parents as possessive individuals or consumers. For pupils the race is on for the prizes of possessing more information and skills than others. The statements of attainment provide the scale against which individual rates of consumption can be compared.

Parents are not viewed· as active participants in an educational process, collaborating with teachers to enable their children to develop their natural powers of understanding. Instead they are viewed as passive beneficiaries of the products of education. Much is made of their freedom to choose an education for their children. But it is the freedom of consumers to buy the product he or she desires and not the freedom of parents to nurture the personal growth of their children.

The dominant theme running through the ERA, is that of competitiveness. It is promoted at every level of education: between pupils, their parents, their teachers and the schools. This theme not only underpins the National Curriculum, but also the infrastructures established by the Act: the opting-out clause, open-enrolment, teacher appraisal, the new powers and responsibilities of school governors. Every aspect of the Act plays its part in promoting competition rather than collaboration. A key feature of the general strategy has been to recognize only those outcomes and goods which can be considered as external to the process of education. In this way education is transformed into a consumer-orientated production process whose effectiveness is promoted by competition within both the consumer and delivery systems.

Consistent with this strategy has been the determination of the government to resist and bypass professional educationalists: teachers and their unions, LEA officials and advisers/inspectors, HM Inspectors, educational researchers and teacher trainers. As we have seen, there has been a tendency for 'the professionals' to try to safeguard ends, values and standards which are internal to educational practices. The intention to restrict the influence of educationalists is surely the point of the clause which requires teachers to seek the permission of the Secretary of State before they attempt any innovations which may not fit the framework established in the Act.

The threat any recognition of internal goods and standards poses for the government is that they imply a commitment to collaborative activities at all levels of education. Pupils develop their powers of understanding, not in social isolation from their peers, but through discussion and the sharing of ideas about problems and issues. Discussion lies at the heart of an educative process. The achievement of individual excellence within this process depends upon the social co-operation of others in establishing the conditions of worthwhile discussion. Moreover, it benefits all the pupils in the class because it enhances their capacities to understand the problem addressed. Competition between individuals to excel in an educational process is contained within a shared recognition that the development of an individual's powers of understanding is a common good because it benefits the whole group.

In failing to recognize the internal values of education the ERA leaves little space for the development of those virtues which characterize the structure of social co-operation within any educative discourse. The Act divorces not only 'standards' from the achievement of 'excellence' in education, but also those virtues which are necessary conditions of such achievement. They constitute the forms of social co-operation implicit in the educative process. Such forms can be sustained in classrooms only if they permeate the ethos of the institutions in which they are situated – schools. These institutions have had to balance supporting an educative process against distributing extrinsic goods upon pupils, e.g. the possession of marketable 'knowledge' and skills. The ERA threatens that balance by sanctioning competitiveness as the dominant and prevailing ethos within and between schools.

It was rather hypocritical for the government to claim, as it did within the text of the Act, that the National Curriculum is concerned with the intellectual, moral and spiritual development of pupils in schools. The logic of technical rationality which permeates it is quite inconsistent with all of these aims. It appears to leave little space for personal development in either its intellectual, moral or spiritual aspects as I shall now attempt to demonstrate.

Academic achievement and personal development

In my earleir account of MacIntyre's analysis of a social practice, I referred to the importance he attributes to locating social practices in some unified vision of the purpose of human life. The account Stenhouse gave of the educational process, as induction into knowledge, needs to be extended at this point. Education is not simply a matter of developing human powers of understanding by inducting students into 'structures of knowledge'. It is about developing these powers in relation to the things which matter in life. Chess is a sophisticated and complex activity which provides opportunities for people to develop a range of complex skills and abilities. But it is nevertheless a game. The problems of chess have little significance as problems of living. It is in relation to the latter that the powers of human understanding must be developed if such a process is to count as an educational one (see Elliott, R., 1973).

Problems of living are not technical problems of discovering the means for achieving ends which can be clearly specified in advance of the solution. They constitute problems about how the various possibilities for action in a situation relate to the over-riding purpose of living. Their solution is not a matter of clarifying the purpose of living and then choosing a course which will achieve it. It is a matter of locating a course of action which is coherent with a unified conception of living. Problems of living arise when situations do not obviously yield courses of action which fit a unified conception of purpose in life. Such problems challenge our prior conceptions of purpose. Any resolution must consist not only of the discovery of an appropriate course of action but also a more developed conception of the purpose of life.

Spiritual development proceeds by resolving problems of living wisely. Wisdom can be defined as the achievement of a sense of unity of purpose in the multiplicity of decisions and acts which constitute a human life. Education is a process which not only inducts into structures of knowledge, but brings those structures into play with the problems of living and utilizing them in the service of wisdom.

The process I have described as spiritual development is an aspect of personal development. It constitutes the primary end of the educational process as a whole. Its realization should not be confined to a slot on the school curriculum called 'religious education' or 'personal and social education'. The existence of such slots exemplifies the displacement of the aims of the whole curriculum to part of that whole. It is evidence of the way in which 'structures of knowledge' have been detached from their educative function of developing our powers to handle the problems of living wisely.

Maxwell (1984) argues that if religion 'is characterized in a broad way as "concern for what is of most value in human existence" then academic inquiry . . . . is essentially a religious enterprise.' (Ch. 4.)

His argument draws on a contrast between two views of intellectual inquiry. Central to one view, that of 'the philosophy of knowledge', is the doctrine that intellectual inquiry must be totally detached from and influenced by the investigator's practical concerns and interests. Central to the other view, that of 'the philosophy of wisdom', is the doctrine that:

> The intellectual progress and success of academic inquiry is to be judged in terms of the extent to which academic work produces and makes available ideas, proposals, arguments, discoveries, techniques that help people achieve what is of value in life in a co-operative and just way. (Ch. 4.)

These two different doctrines, according to Maxwell, have radically different implications for education. Intellectual inquiry shaped by 'the philosophy of knowledge' posits two quite separate types of learning: 'On the one hand there is academic learning; on the other hand there is learning how to live.' However, if intellectual inquiry is shaped by the 'philosophy of wisdom', the dichotomy disappears: 'Academic learning *is* learning about how to live.'

If we construe education as a process of induction into knowledge that is related to the things which matter for living then its intrinsic goods can be classified according to three of its interrelated dimensions of personal development: the intellectual, moral and spiritual. The intellectual goods consist of the development of the powers of human understanding in relation to the problems of living. The spiritual goods consist of the development of wisdom through the exercise of these intellectual powers, and the moral goods consist of those virtues or attitudes which are necessary conditions for developing the powers of the understanding and discovering solutions to the fundamental problems of living.

In spite of its espoused aims of promoting the intellectual, moral and spiritual development of pupils the national curriculum detaches academic learning from 'learning how to live' and at best caters for the latter in lower-status slots on the curriculum. Separating 'academic learning' from 'learning about how to live' makes it easier to construe knowledge as information and skills rather than as dynamic structures within which to think about the problems of living. It also makes the achievements of learning easier and less costly 'things' to test and compare.

The task group in science appears to have struggled hard to accommodate the idea of targets to their conception of a worthwhile scientific education. They consistently argued that induction into science should not be detached from the study of practical problems of living which raise questions about fundamental human values. The maths group appears to have wanted to adopt a similar line although they were not to my knowledge so explicit about the sorts of practical problems they had in mind – whether their concern was with the application of maths to technical problems or with its application to more fundamental problems in real life. A similar issue has underpinned the debates surrounding the work of the history and geography task groups concerning the emphasis to be placed on factual knowledge in relation to an understanding of human situations.

In the *Independent* (17 August 1988) Simon Midgely reported that the Secretary of State had 'serious reservations about the weight both groups attribute to the importance of children applying scientific and mathematical knowledge in the real world.' Evidently he felt 'that more emphasis still needs to be placed on basic knowledge and understanding in each subject.' It would not be too presumptuous to interpret the demand for more emphasis on 'basic knowledge and understanding' as a demand for more emphasis on specific items of information and facts. As I suggested previously, the pressure is towards abstracting and isolating information and skills from their appropriate location in an educative process. What the government have failed to realize is that the emphasis they wanted actually undermines planning a curriculum which is capable of fostering personal development in each of the dimensions cited as aims in the Act: namely, the intellectual, moral and spiritual. It is to the credit of the National Curriculum Council responsible for implementation that it has attempted to overcome this separation through its guidelines on how to handle cross-curricular themes.

In his article Midgely referred to the government's concern to lift the performance of average and below-average children, 'the bottom 40 per cent'. The concern is shared by the task groups. However, there may be in operation two different diagnoses of the problem. The government appears to assume that these pupils lack 'basic' information and skills because they have not been taught them systematically. The idea of specifying them as targets is a device for ensuring that they will be in future. The alternative diagnosis, which may well find subscribers in the task groups, is that the 'basics' have not been learned. And this is not necessarily because they were not taught, but because pupils were not required to learn them in a context which activated and challenged their intellectual powers in relation to the things that really matter in life. In other words, such learning made little sense because these pupils could not fit it into any meaningful context of living. Perhaps they were less willing than their more 'achieving' peers to spend time and effort learning meaningless information and skills. If the second diagnosis is correct, then the specification of attainment targets will do little for the bottom 40 per cent.

What is required is a national plan which starts, not with target specifications, but with a map of the dimensions of human experience which matter for contemporary living. The next step would be to select content to exemplify problems, dilemmas and issues of living which experience confronts in these dimensions. *Hamlet*'s educational value primarily lies not in its instrumentality for learning literacy skills, but in the fact that it speaks to the human condition.

Such a curriculum map of the content of education would specify not information to be learned but situations to be addressed. It is only when this kind of map has been developed that we are in a position to select knowledge structures which might enable pupils to develop their understanding of 'life situations' and to select those specific items of information and technical skills which need to be acquired in the process of such development.

Stenhouse argued that, from the standpoint of the 'process model', the starting-point for curriculum design was the mapping of content rather than of objectives. From this point of view the procedures embedded in the development of the National Curriculum are bound to treat content as of instrumental value. Rather than set up task groups to define subject targets prior to the specification of programmes of study and cross-curricular guidelines by the Curriculum Council, a process-model approach would have begun with a map of the kinds of situations to be addressed in developing the powers of the understanding, and in acquiring relevant information and skills. And there is no reason why parents, employers and members of the public generally could not be involved in developing such a map. It is a task for society as a whole. The task of the professional educators is a different one, which I shall now turn to.

Earlier I suggested that Stenhouse's process model made explicit in a coherent form many of the ideas already implicit in the curriculum-reform practices of teachers during the 60s in innovatory secondary modern schools. These teachers were also trying to resolve the problem of underachieving pupils. I have claimed that their practices embodied a curriculum theory which consisted of a cluster of interrelated ideas about education, learning, curriculum and teaching. The key elements of this theory were as follows:

1 Education is a process in which pupils develop their intellectual powers by utilizing public structures of knowledge in constructing personal understandings of life situations. Within an educational process differing understandings of the same situation may manifest similar intellectual powers. It is only when knowledge is exclusively regarded as information to be reproduced through memory learning that understanding is presumed to consist of a uniform learning outcome.

2 Learning involves the active construction rather than the passive reproduction of meaning.
3 Learning is assessed in terms of the development of intellectual powers manifested in its outcomes, rather than in terms of the match between predetermined performance standards and performance outcomes. The educational quality of the latter can be described and judged but not standardized as performance indicators and measured.
4 Teaching aims to enable or facilitate the development of pupils' natural powers of understanding (rather than to produce certain predetermined performance outcomes). It is concerned with establishing enabling conditions.
5 The criteria for evaluating teaching differ from those for evaluating learning. In evaluating teaching the criteria employed refer to conditions which enable pupils to develop their powers. But these are not causal conditions. They establish opportunities for pupils to develop their powers of understanding. Whether pupils take these opportunities is another matter.

In evaluating learning the criteria employed refer to qualities of mind actually manifested in the performance of pupils. What counts as useful curriculum knowledge cannot be determined in advance of the pedagogical process. It is determined on the basis of teachers' own reflective deliberations as they select and organize theories, concepts and ideas in response to pupils' search for personal meaning. 'Structures of knowledge', information and skills can only be preselected as resources for learning. The appropriateness of these resources for developing pupils' powers in relation to life situations can be tested only in a pedagogical process of teacher-based action research. Curriculum development and teaching are not two distinct processes. The former is a dimension of the latter.

This curriculum theory, embedded in curriculum reform practices initiated by teachers, is consistent with the theory of education I have expounded in this chapter. It also explains the emphasis Stenhouse placed on the development of teachers as curriculum researchers, and his slogan that 'there can be no curriculum development without teacher development.'

The theory enables us to develop further an alternative approach to the development of the National Curriculum. I have already suggested that a process model would begin with a societal mapping of the kinds of life situations pupils need to address in developing their powers of understanding. The next stage, for the National Curriculum Council, would be to review all areas of knowledge in the light of the problems, dilemmas and issues framework. This would not only entail revisions to the content of established curriculum subjects but the introduction of quite new subject areas, e.g. medicine, law or architecture. We might end up with a rather different set of subject areas to those proposed in the ERA.

The next questions would be:

- How do we know that the selections of knowledge are useful?
- What is the best way of organizing this knowledge for pedagogical purposes?

These questions can only be answered on the basis of teacher experiment and reflection in classrooms. Moreover, it is unlikely that one would be able to secure agreement about what counts as useful knowledge and how it is best organized for pedagogical purposes. This is because so much will depend on the different classroom and school contexts in which teachers operate. What constitutes useful knowledge in one context may prove useless in another. And what constitutes a pedagogically supportive form of curriculum organization in one context may undermine the quality of the pedagogy in another.

Within the process model there are limits to what can be nationally specified. What is important is the concept of the National Curriculum as a resource to support reflective pedagogical practice in schools, and the establishment of mechanisms by which central government can continuously modify its curriculum map in the light of feedback from teachers and schools.

The whole enterprise ultimately rests on the quality of teachers. The kind of curriculum development process I have outlined certainly assumes the existence of a teaching profession capable of improving the quality of education through reflective pedagogical practice. But then on my account there is no alternative way of improving education. The alternative proposed in the Reform Act is to abandon the concept of an educational practice and to transform schooling into a production process in which teachers are deprofessionalized into technical operatives administering prescribed treatments in the light of the prescribed product specifications. The idea of teachers as professionals only makes sense within a context in which education is viewed as a social practice.

References

Altricher, H. and Posch, P. (1989). 'Does the grounded theory approach offer a guiding paradigm for teacher research?' *Cambridge Journal of Education*, vol. 19, no. 1.

Aoki, T. T. (1984). 'Competence in teaching as instrumental and practical action: a critical analysis' in Short, E. C. (ed.) *Competence: Inquiries into its Meaning and Acquisition in Educational Settings*. Lanham, NY, and London, University Press of America.

Block, M. (1985). 'From cognition to ideology' in Forden, R. (ed.) *Power and Knowledge: Anthropological and Sociological Approaches*. Edinburgh, Scottish Academic Press.

Boothroyd, D. and Burbidge, S. (1988). *Teacher Appraisal?* London Borough of Enfield, Enfield Teachers Centre.

Boyle, N. (1988). 'Understanding Thatcherism', *New Blackfriars*. Summer 1988.

Carr, W. and Kemmis, S. (1983). *Becoming Critical: Knowing through Action Research*. Victoria, Australia, Deakin University Press, ch. 5, 132–41.

——(1986). *Becoming Critical: Education, Knowledge and Action Research*, Lewes, Falmer Press.

Carson, T. and Couture, J.-C. (eds.) (1988). *Collaborative Action Research: Experience and Reflections*, Improvement of Instruction Series, Monograph no. 18, Alberta Teachers' Association.

Committee of Vice-Chancellors and Principals/Association of University Teachers (CVCP/AUT) (1987). *Career Development and Staff Appraisal Procedures for Academic Related Staff*. London, CVCP.

DES (Department of Education and Science) (1983). *Teaching Quality*, Cmnd 8836. London, Her Majesty's Stationery Office.

DES/ACAS (Department of Education and Science/ACAS Independent Panel) (1986). *Report of the Appraisal and Training Working Group*.

Doll, W. E. (1984). 'Developing competence' in Short, E. (ed.) *Competence: Inquiries into its Meaning and Acquisition in Educational Settings*. Lanham, NY, and London, University Press of America.

Dreyfus, S. E. (1981). *Four Models v. Human Situational Understanding: Inherent Limitations on the Modelling of Business Expertise*. US Air Force Office of Scientific Research, Contract No. F49620-79-C-0063.

Ebbutt, D. and Elliott, J. (eds.) (1985). *Issues in Teaching for Understanding*. London, Longman/Schools Curriculum Development Committee (SCDC).

Elliott, J. (1976–7). 'Developing hypotheses about classrooms from teachers' practical constructs: an account of the work of the Ford Teaching Project'. *Interchange*, vol. 7, no. 2. Ontario Institute for Studies in Education.

——(1981a). 'The teacher as researcher within award bearing courses' in Alexander, R. J. and Ellis, J. W. (eds.) *Advanced Study for Teachers*, Teacher Education Study Group, Society for Research into Higher Education, distributed by Naferton Books.

——(c. 1981b). 'How teachers learn' in Chambers, P. (ed.) *Making INSET Work – Myth or Reality?*, Bradford, Faculty of Contemporary Studies, Bradford College.

——(1983a). 'A curriculum for the study of human affairs: the contribution of Lawrence Stenhouse'. *Journal of Curriculum Studies*, vol. 15, no. 2, 105–23.

——(1983b). 'Self-evaluation, professional development and accountability' in Galton, M. and Moon, R. (ed.), *Changing Schools . . . Changing Curriculum*. London, Harper & Row, ch. 15.

——(1985). 'Educational action research' in Nisbet, J. (ed.) *World Yearbook of Education 1985: Research, Policy and Practice*. London, Kogan Page.

——(1987a). 'Educational theory, practical philosophy and action research', *British Journal of Educational Studies*, 25, 2.

——(1987b). 'Knowledge, power and appraisal', paper delivered to the Annual Conference of the British Educational Research Association. Norwich, Centre for Applied Research in Education, School of Education, University of East Anglia.

——(1988). 'The great appraisal debate: some perspectives for research' in Eggins, H. (ed.) *Restructuring Higher Education*, Milton Keynes, Open University Press.

——(1989a). 'Teacher evaluation and teaching as a moral science' in Holly, M. L. and McLoughlin, C. S. (eds.) *Perspectives on Teacher Professional Development*. London and New York, Falmer Press.

——(1989b). 'Educational theory and the professional learning of teachers'. *Cambridge Journal of Education*, vol. 1, no. 1.

Elliott, J. (1990). 'Teachers as researchers: implications for supervision and teacher education', *Teaching and Teaching Education*, vol. 6, no. 1.

Elliott, J. *et al.* (1979). 'Implementing school-based action research: some hypotheses'. *Cambridge Journal of Education*, vol. 9, no. 1.

Elliott, J. and Adelman, C. (1976). *Innovation at the Classroom Level: A Case Study of the Ford Teaching Project*, Course CE203. Milton Keynes, Open University.

Elliott, J. and Ebbutt, D. (eds.) (1986). *Case Studies in Teaching for Understanding*, Cambridge Institute of Education.

Elliott, J. and MacDonald, B. (eds.) (1975). *People in Classrooms*, Occasional Publications no. 2, Norwich, Centre for Applied Research in Education, University of East Anglia.

Elliott, J. with Partington, D. (1975). 'Three points of view in the classroom', Ford Teaching Project Documents, Norwich, University of East Anglia.

Elliott, R. K. (1973). 'Education and human being' in Brown, S. C. (ed.) *Philosophers Discuss Education*, London, Macmillan, 1975.

Foucault M. (1980). Gordon, Colin (ed.) *Power/Knowledge: Selected Interviews and Other Writings 1972–1977*. Brighton, Harvester Press.

Fromm, E. (1976). *To Have or To Be?*. London, Abacus/Sphere, 1979.

Gadamer, H. G. (1975). *Truth and Method*. New York, Seabury.

Giroux, H. (1983). *Theory and Resistance in Education: A Pedagogy for the Opposition*. London, Heinemann Educational, 107–11.

Handy, C. (1984). 'Education for management outside business' in Goodlad, S. (ed.) *Education for the Professions*, London, Society for Research into Higher Education and NFER/Nelson.

Hargreaves, D. H. (1982). *The Challenge for the Comprehensive School: Culture, Curriculum and Community*. London, Boston and Henley, Routledge & Kegan Paul.

Hewton, E. (1988). 'Teacher appraisal: the present position', *Education*, 8, January.

The Humanities Curriculum Project: An Introduction (1970), revised by Jean Rudduck, 1985. London, Schools Council Publications.

ILEA (1977). *Keeping the School Under Review*. London, Inner London Education Authority.

James, M. (1982). 'Institutional self-evaluation' in *Approaches to Evaluation*, Part II, Course EC64 on Curriculum Evaluation and Assessment in Educational Institutions, Block 2. Milton Keynes, Open University.

James, M. and Ebbutt, D. (1980). 'Problems of engaging in research in one's own school' in Nixon, J. (ed.) *A Teacher's Guide to Action Research*, Grant McIntyre.

Jessup, G. (1989). 'The emerging model of vocational education and training' in Burke, J. W. (ed.) *Competency Based Education and Training*. London, New York and Philadelphia, Falmer Press.

Johnson, H. C. (1984). 'Teacher competence: an historical analysis' in Short, E. C. (ed.) *Competence, Inquiries into Its Meaning and Acquisition in Educational Settings*, Lanham, NY and London, University Press of America.

Kemmis, S. (1980). 'Action research in retrospect and prospect', mimeo presented at the Annual General Meeting of the Australian Association for Research in Education, Sydney, November 1980.

Kemmis, S. and others (1981). *The Action Research Planner*, Victoria, Australia, Deakin University.

Kerr, J. (1968). 'The problem of curriculum reform' in Kerr, J. (ed.) *Changing the Curriculum*, London, University of London Press.

Klemp, G. O. (1977). *Three Factors of Success in the World of Work: Implications for Curriculum in Higher Education*. Boston, McBer & Co.

Kroath, F. (1989). 'How do teachers change their practical theories?'. *Cambridge Journal of Education*, vol. 19, no. 1.

McCarthy, C. (1978). *The Critical Theory of Jurgen Habermas*. London, Hutchinson, 187–93.

McClelland, D. C. (1973). 'Testing for competence rather than for intelligence', *American Psychologist*, 28, 1–14.

——(1976). *A Guide to Job Competency Assessment*. Boston, McBer & Co.

MacDonald, B. (1970). 'The evaluation of the Humanities Curriculum Project: a holistic approach', paper presented to American Educational Research Association, New York. Published in *Theory into Practice*, Norwich, CARE OCC Publ., University of East Anglia.

——(1974). 'Evaluation and the control of education' in Tawney, D. (ed.) *Curriculum Evaluation Today: Trends and Implications*. London, Macmillan.

MacDonald, B. (1978). 'Accountability, standards, and the process of schooling' in Becher, T. and Maclure, S. (eds) *Accountability in Education*, National Foundation for Educational Research (NFER).

MacIntyre, A. (1981). *After Virtue: A Study in Moral Theory*. London, Duckworh, ch. 14.

Maxwell, N. (1984). *From Knowledge to Wisdom*. Oxford, Blackwell, ch. 4.

Pearson, H. T. (1984). 'Competence: an historical analysis' in Short, E. C. *Competence: Inquiries into its Meaning and Acquisition in Educational Settings*. Lanham, NY and London, University Press of America.

Peters, R. S. (1959). *Authority, Responsibility and Education*. London: Allen & Unwin.

——(1968). 'Must an educator have an aim?' in MacMillan, C. B. and Nelson, T. (eds) *Concepts of Teaching*. Chicago, Rand McNally.

Reid, W. (1978). *Thinking about the Curriculum*. London, Routledge.

Runciman, W. G. (1983). *A Treatise on Social Theory, Volume One: The Methodology of Social Theory*. Cambridge University Press.

Russell, T. (1988). 'From pre-service teacher education to first year of teaching: a study of theory and practice' in Calderhead, J. (ed.) *Teachers' Professional Learning*. London, New York and Philadelphia, Falmer Press.

Sanger, J. (ed.) (1989). *The Teaching, Handling Information and Learning Project*. Library and Information Research Report 67. London, British Library.

Schon, D. (1983). *The Reflective Practitioner*. London, Temple Smith.

——(1987). *Educating the Reflective Practitioner*. London, Jossey-Bass.

Schwab, J. J. (1970). *The Practical: A Language for Curriculum*. Washington, D.C. National Education Association, Centre for the Study of Instruction.

Simons, H. (1978). 'Process evaluation in practice in schools', mimeo, Curriculum Studies Department, University of London Institute of Education.

——(1985). 'Against the rules: procedural problems in school self-evaluation', *Curriculum Perspectives*, vol. 5, no. 2.

——(1987). *Getting to Know Schools in a Democracy: The Politics and Process of Evaluation*. London, New York and Philadelphia, Falmer Press.

Somekh, B. (1988). 'Collaborative action-research: working together towards professional development', mimeo, Norwich, Centre for Applied Research in Education, University of East Anglia.

Spencer, L. M. (1979). *Identifying, Measuring, and Training Soft Skill Competencies Which Predict Performance in Professional, Managerial and Human Service Jobs*. Boston, McBer & Co.

Stenhouse, L. (1968). 'The Humanities Curriculum Project'. *Journal of Curriculum Studies*, vol. 23, no. 1.

——(1971). 'The Humanities Curriculum Project: the rationale'. *Theory into Practice*, 10, 154–62.

——(1975). *An Introduction to Curriculum Research and Development*. London, Heinemann.

——(1978). 'Case study and case records: towards a contemporary history of education'. *British Educational Research Journal*, vol. 4, no. 2.

Suffolk County Council Education Department (1985). *Those Having Torches – Teacher Appraisal: A Study*. Ipswich, County Hall, St Andrew Street.

——(1987). *Teacher Appraisal: A Practical Guide.* Ipswich, County Hall, St Andrew Street.

Tuxworth, E. (1989). 'Competence based education and training: background and origins' in Burke, J. W. (ed.) *Competency Based Education and Training.* London, New York and Philadelphia, Falmer Press.

Walker, R. and Adelman, C. (1975). *Guide to Classroom Observation.* London, Methuen.

Whitehead, J. (1989). 'Creating a living educational theory from questions of the kind, "How do I improve my practice?"'. *Cambridge Journal of Education.*, vol. 19, no. 1, 1989.

Winter, R. (1982). 'Dilemma analysis: a contribution to methodology for action research'. *Cambridge Journal of Education*, vol. 12, no. 3.

Wolf, A. (1989). 'Can competence and knowledge mix?' in Burke, J. W. (ed.) *Competency Based Education and Training.* London, New York and Philadelphia, Falmer Press.

Zeichner, K. M. (1981). 'Reflective teaching and field based experience in teacher education'. *Interchange*, 12, 4, 1–22.

——(1983). 'Alternative paradigms of teacher education'. *Journal of Teacher Education*, 34, 3, 3–9.

Index